PHAIDON GUIDE TO
GLASS

PHAIDON GUIDE TO
GLASS

FELICE MEHLMAN

PHAIDON · OXFORD

Frontispiece   A cameo glass and gilt bronze peony lamp by Émile Gallé, c. 1900.

Published by Phaidon Press Ltd, Littlegate House, St Ebbe's Street, Oxford

Planned, produced and © 1982 by Equinox (Oxford) Ltd

British Library Cataloguing in Publication Data
Mehlman, Felice
    Phaidon guide to glass.
    1. Glassware – Collectors and collecting
    I. Title
    748.2   NK1504

    ISBN 0–7148–2202–7

Design by Adrian Hodgkins

Composition in Univers by Keyspools Ltd, Golborne, Lancashire

Illustrations originated by Contemporary Lithoplates Ltd, London and Siviter Smith Offset Ltd, Birmingham

Printed in Hungary by Kossuth Nyomda, Budapest

CONTENTS

PREFACE

For over 3,000 years, glass-makers have created a magnificent range of pieces both functional and decorative, and so it is particularly with the collector in mind that this book has been planned and written. The majority of books describe the development of glass solely in a chronological and geographical context. The main section of this guide, however, is categorised in terms of the *objects* which have been produced. I have chosen this different approach not only to indicate the great variety of pieces still available to the collector – from traditional drinking glasses to jewellery, mirrors and paperweights – but also to isolate and emphasise specific forms and functions which a regional survey can only mention in passing.

A short history of each of the principal manufacturing countries or regions is also included, together with an introduction which describes the materials and methods employed in glass-making. Although it was not felt appropriate to discuss contemporary productions in detail, a section has been devoted to popular decorative styles of the 19th and early 20th centuries. The chapter on collecting seeks to provide beginners and enthusiasts with specific information on how to examine and care for pieces, with advice on restoration, prices, fakes and reproductions. Would-be collectors have sometimes found glass a bewildering and complex field, an impression which has been fostered to a large extent by many books and articles published on the subject. It is hoped that this chapter will encourage the enthusiast to obtain practical advice and experience, and dispel some of the myths which appear to have inhibited collectors in the past.

Line drawings provide additional information to illustrate important technical and stylistic features, and should be referred to in conjunction with the relevant accompanying text. The photographs, many of which have been specially commissioned and are published for the first time, illustrate objects chosen from specialist dealers and salerooms over a period of about a year. Famous museum pieces have been mentioned in context, but as they appear frequently in standard reference books their illustrations have been excluded here.

Finally, I am grateful to Chris Sheppard, Andy Burne, Maureen Thompson, Martin Mortimer, and Perran Wood of Sotheby's for their invaluable assistance. But I particularly thank my husband Stephen for his encouragement, patience and advice on the writing of this book.

Felice Mehlman

A glass-blower at work, breathing into his blow-pipe, and simultaneously twisting the gather to make it even and symmetrical. The long arms of the "chair" can be seen to the left, designed to support the pipe while the bubble is swung and rotated into shape – the next stage of manufacture. From *The Book of English Trades*, London, 1821.

INTRODUCTION

WHAT GLASS IS

Glass is an artificial substance which has been employed for nearly 3,500 years to create a wide and varied range of objects for both domestic and industrial purposes. It is a highly versatile and flexible material, easily manipulated and shaped when hot. Clear and colourless like rock-crystal, opaque, or richly coloured to simulate semi-precious stones, glass is able to sustain numerous forms of decoration including cutting, engraving, gilding, enamelling, trailing and other applied ornamentation. It is a medium for artistic expression, but the evolution of its forms and decorative styles must be credited not only to the skills and talents of the glass-worker, but also to those of the chemist, for his discovery of new and improved "metals" and colours.

Glass is created by fusing a silica such as sand, quartz or flint, with an alkali such as soda or potash. The latter acts as a flux, assisting the silica to melt, and encouraging the batch, or mixture, to combine more readily. The silica and alkaline flux are the basic ingredients common to all glass, but other substances are also added to the batch to make the final product more durable and attractive – such as lime (for stability), magnesium (to counter the effects of any impurities present in the sand by making the glass clear and colourless), lead oxide (for weight and brilliance) and a variety of metal oxides (for colour). The main constituents of glass are discussed briefly below, as are several of the principal formulae which have been employed for centuries by glass-makers, and which have altered little since their discovery.

The silica

This is the most important ingredient, forming about 60–70% of the batch, and employed in the form of sand, sandstone, quartz rock or flint stones. Sand, found on beaches and inland river-beds, was obtained readily by early glass-makers in places such as Lorraine in France, regions of Germany and Bohemia, and in Kent, Norfolk and the Sussex Weald of England. The Venetians crushed the white quartz pebbles of the Ticino river-bed for their silica, and the English also used burnt and powdered flints for this purpose. It was important to use a silica which was largely free from impurities, as sand with a high iron content, for example, could have disastrous effects on the final colour of the glass, tinting or discolouring it easily. The result of using an unrefined silica was what is known as common "bottle glass", a coarse glass of dark green or brown. For the manufacture of fine quality glass, the sand had to be prepared carefully – washed and heated to remove impurities – and free of any irregularly sized grains.

The alkaline flux

Fifteen to 20% of the batch took the form of potash or soda ash, which was obtained by burning certain species of plants and trees. Soda (sodium carbonate) was employed for glass-making in countries such as Egypt (in the form of natron), throughout the Near East (where it was known as *roquetta*), in Spain (where *barrilla*, as it was called, was obtained from glasswort and exported widely from Alicante) and in Venice. In northern Europe soda was obtained by burning kelp (seaweed) in the Normandy region of France, in Norway, Scotland and parts of England. Potash (potassium carbonate) was used as an alternative to soda when access to marine plants was difficult, and thus formed an essential glass-making ingredient in inland forest regions of Europe as it could be made by burning local supplies of either bracken and other ferns (employed in France for *verre de fougère*), or beechwood, pine and oak (used in Germany for *Waldglas*).

Soda is the more effective flux. It can fuse the sand and other ingredients at relatively low temperatures and it possesses highly plastic qualities in a molten state, permitting easy manipulation. Thus, the soda glass of the Mediterranean region, including Venetian soda-lime *cristallo*, frequently demonstrates elaborate glass trailing and a range of fanciful shapes, contrasting with the heavy northern European potash glass which is much better suited to decorative cutting and engraving. Today, soda and potash continue to be used as glass-making ingredients.

Other ingredients

The remaining 10–20% of the batch usually includes one or more of the ingredients lime, lead oxide and borax. Lime is a good stabilising element, producing a light and relatively inexpensive glass, used commonly in the making of bottles, window panes and, later, electric light bulbs. Small quantities of lime are present in the tree and plant ashes mentioned above, or it can be added in the form of chalk, crushed to a powder, as used in Germany and Bohemia from the late 17th century onwards. The use of lead oxide was developed by George Ravenscroft during the 1670s to produce a superior "metal" which was durable, brilliant and weighty. These qualities made it an ideal medium for decorative cutting and for use in optics. The crystalline salt borax occurs naturally in certain minerals, and was used initially as a flux for early lead glass production; more recently it has been employed in the "Pyrex" range of cooking wares, for its heat- and shock-resistant qualities.

Before the advent of analytical chemistry during the late 18th century, the mixing of the ingredients was a haphazard process, apparently controlled more by factors such as

INTRODUCTION

experience and luck than by design. If the proportions were incorrect, the resultant glass might appear "crizzled" or diseased, and be prone to deterioration. Crizzling occurred frequently during experimental stages of glass-making (i.e. setting up a new factory, or creating a new metal); this can be seen in, for example, the early lead glass wares of George Ravenscroft, or the initial productions of Chinese "imperial glass" during the late 17th century.

HOW GLASS IS MADE

From the important invention of the iron blow-pipe during the early Christian era until the Industrial Revolution little progress was made in glass-making techniques. Indeed, many of the methods devised by the Romans for the execution of decorative and artistic wares were forgotten or lost for centuries following the decline of the Roman empire.

Briefly outlined below are the *main* processes which were employed for the manufacture of vessels and other objects from the 1st century AD onwards. A discussion of the techniques used before the introduction of blowing appears in the chapter on Egyptian glass (see pp. 30–34). Window and mirror-making methods are described on pp. 202–9.

The furnace

The silica, alkaline flux and other selected ingredients were mixed together into a dry powder (the batch). Pieces of broken glass of the same composition as the raw materials (the cullet) were frequently added to this mixture to facilitate fusion, and to make efficient use of waste materials. Until recently, it was common for the alkali and part of the sand to be pre-heated and partly fused before being added to the final ingredients. This "frit" could be used immediately, or reserved for future use. The batch was placed in a crucible or fire-clay pot, to be heated and fused. Several pots were placed together (probably in a circle above the central source of heat) in the furnace, which could be divided into sections for fritting, melting the batch and annealing. The top of the furnace was usually designed in the shape of a dome, to deflect the heat downwards in order to surround the crucibles with a constant temperature. Wood was employed as fuel in England until the early 17th century, when its use was prohibited by royal proclamation due to depleted supplies and it was replaced by pit-coal. Elsewhere in Europe wood continued to be used until the 19th century. Peat was a common fuel in Denmark and Silesia during the 18th and 19th centuries respectively, and more recently oil, gas and electricity have been employed. Temperatures of between 1300 and 1500°C are needed to fuse the batch, and the entire melting process could take up

A glass furnace, showing a range of activities: the worker on the far right heats his blow-pipe so that the hot glass will adhere to it, while the gatherer to his left rolls and twists the glass on the marver. Behind them, a glass-blower breathes through the mouthpiece of the pipe to create a bubble. In the foreground, various blow-pipes (A), shears (D), and moulds (E) lay ready for use, surrounded by bits of broken glass which may be added to the next batch and re-melted. The finished wares are stored in a crate, to be taken away and sold by the glass seller depicted in the background, who carries his large load to town. From G. Agricola, *De re metallica*, Basle, 1556.

An unusual and curious red glass footed beaker in the filigree style, possibly dating to the late 17th century, of Venetian manufacture. Note the small holes caused by burst bubbles and cutting marks made by the shears – obvious errors, but ones which appear to have deterred the glass-maker little from completing his work; $3\frac{1}{4}$in.

to 48 hours. During this time, impurities rising to the surface of the mixture could be skimmed off (from an opening at the shoulder of the pot, where the hot glass was later removed for blowing). Once a molten state was achieved and the ingredients were properly fused, the glass was ready to be shaped.

Today, the pot furnace described above is still used for glass manufacture (each fire-clay pot can hold up to one ton of glass) or alternatively a tank furnace is employed, where the mixture is melted in a large tank containing up to 2,000 tons of glass.

Glass blowing

An iron blow-pipe or a pontil, about 6 feet in length, was first heated at its thickened end so that the glass would adhere to it, and then plunged into a crucible to collect a "gather" or blob of hot glass. By twisting and dipping the rod into the mixture several times, a sufficient quantity of glass could be amassed. The gather was then rolled onto a "marver" (a marble or iron slab, derived from the French word *marbre* meaning marble) to make it smooth and symmetrical, and then re-heated and blown into a bubble or "paraison" by breathing through the wooden mouthpiece at the other end of the pipe. The process of re-heating and blowing could be repeated several times, until the desired size, shape and thickness was achieved. If the gather had been collected on a pontil, it would be transferred to a blow-pipe for blowing. The master glass-blower or "gaffer" (see below) would be seated at his "chair", designed with long arms on either side on which he could rest his pipe horizontally, rolling it to and fro with one hand and with the other shaping it with pincers, tongs and shears. In between he could rise to swing and rotate the pipe, keeping the glass in constant movement to prevent it sagging, and making use of the centrifugal force to give it shape. Eventually, the bubble, now given its basic shape, was transferred to a pontil – a long rod with no hole through it – and the glass completed. The making of a drinking glass or other vessel demanded the close cooperation of several glass-blowers – one to make a stem, another a foot – and the various pieces were all joined together in the last stages, at the same degree of heat and fluidity, and given the final touches by the gaffer. Alternatively, the gather could be blown directly into a mould (consisting, initially, of one or two pieces, and later, three or four pieces for complex designs) of carved wood, stone or clay, or (more recently) metal, so that the finished object would assume the shape and pattern of the interior of the mould. After cooling, the mould was opened and the blow-pipe cracked off; if desired, the object could be expanded by further blowing.

Annealing
All glass, whether made by hand or machine, must be annealed. This is a process whereby the finished article is re-heated in a special furnace, known as a *lehr*, and subsequently cooled – gradually and uniformly – to relieve the object of internal stress, and reduce the risk of fracture.

Industrialised production
Both the methods described above, that is free-blowing and mould-blowing, have been practised continuously since the days of the Romans, and have changed little since that time, still being ultimately dependent upon the skills and ingenuity of the workforce. During the 19th century, however, new machine-operated methods were developed in the U.S.A (and soon brought to Europe) whereby the process of blowing into metal moulds from a source of compressed air could be mechanically controlled; it was used in the manufacture of bottles (such as the well-known "Coca-cola" bottle) and electric light bulbs. The latter were hand-blown until 1917, when an automatic machine was developed, capable of producing 10,000 bulbs per day. In 1926, advancing technology raised this number to over 24,000 bulbs per day.

Mould-pressing was another mechanised method of manufacture, introduced in about 1827 (see American Glass, p. 94), whereby the molten glass was poured into a metal mould and "pressed" by a plunger from which it took its shape and decoration. Mould-pressing, either hand-operated or fully automatic, was initially used to simulate the effect of hand-cut ornamentation, and the mass production of this type of ware made it a cheap and attractive alternative.

The glass-makers

The factory or glass-house was usually staffed by a large workforce. Individuals were assigned to a specific job and supervised by the glass-house master (*maître verrier*) whose responsibility it was to control what was being made, in which quantities and by whom, and to mix the batch. The gaffer and other glass-blowers were supported by a large ancillary staff of furnace-builders, pot-makers, fuel-carriers and stokers.

Working at the lamp

For making small glass objects such as toys, trinkets and beads, the craftsman would work "at the lamp", where rods of annealed glass could be heated in the concentrated flame of an oil lamp (or, later, a Bunsen burner) and shaped by tools. Lamp-work was usually carried out in a glass-maker's workshop, as opposed to the factory, and it has been practised since Roman times. During the late 19th century, the process was also adapted to European "art glass" production.

HOW GLASS IS COLOURED

The techniques of colouring glass were discovered at least 1,500 years prior to the manufacture of a relatively clear, colourless glass by the Romans. Among the ancient Egyptian vessels which have survived are many in a rich range of opaque colours. Egyptian glass-makers knew how to create various shades of blue – a pervasive and highly favoured colour – as well as green, yellow, violet, white, black and bright red. The reasons for their marked preference for coloured wares were firstly, to disguise the natural green, brown and purple tints brought about by impurities, and, secondly, to imitate semi-precious stones which were greatly prized. During the Roman period when the technique of glass-blowing had been mastered to produce a range of thin-walled hollow vessels, the normal repertoire of colours was extended to include a "colourless" glass, created by the addition of manganese oxide. The Roman author Pliny described the latter as being the most treasured glass of all. However, it is probable that a true clarity of tone was not achieved and that pieces were still slightly tinted by the impurities present in the sand. Since the fall of the western Roman empire at the end of the 5th century, relatively few new shades have been discovered (many of these only recently); the processes (outlined below) used in their manufacture have altered little during the course of time.

INTRODUCTION

Pair of "imperial yellow" Chinese vases of slender baluster form, inscribed with a poem and the emperor's seal mark. This important colour was reserved initially for the court, although by the 19th century its use was less exclusive. Qianlong period (1736–96).

The production of coloured glass is achieved by four basic methods: i) using unrefined glass-making ingredients in which impurities are present naturally, so that the resultant metal appears green or brown in tone (for example, "bottle glass"); ii) adding to the batch a variety of metal oxides, sulphides or selenides in solution so that they dissolve, imparting different colours; iii) adding to the metal coloured particles which are dispersed throughout, so that the object assumes the shade of these tinted specks (as in aventurine glass, containing oxidised metallic flakes, in imitation of aventurine quartz with its tiny inclusions of mica); iv) "striking": adding minute metallic particles (smaller than those in the above method) to the glass which is then re-heated, the colour created resulting from the interaction between the particles and the "metal" of the glass. The process of re-heating must be controlled carefully, as the colour of the glass can change dramatically as the temperature varies. This technique of colouring was practised in the making of "gold ruby" glass, developed by the chemist Johann Kunckel during the 1670s (see p. 65), in which microscopic particles of gold chloride were added

14

to the metal to yield a rich ruby hue. If the glass was not heated enough, the gold particles remained too small and inconsequential, resulting in a pale yellow tint (known as "unstruck") and if over-heating occurred, the particles expanded to produce a blue tint ("overstruck").

All methods of colouring glass rely ultimately on the skills of the glass-maker and his control over factors such as furnace conditions, the quality of the selected materials and their use in correct proportion. For example, the addition of copper oxide to the glass substance can produce two very different colours, according to the type of furnace employed. In a reducing atmosphere (i.e. non-oxidising and rich in carbon monoxide) copper yields a red shade, but in an oxidising environment a blue or green tint is achieved.

The colouring of glass by the addition of metal oxides has been practised since the earliest days of glass manufacture, and experimentation with new materials and combinations has slowly brought about the emergence of a few novel shades and a variety of colour effects. Listed here are the most commonly employed colouring agents.

Antimony. Known to glass-makers of ancient Egypt to produce yellow, and to create opacity in other shades.

Amethyst decanter bottle with decoration "nipt-diamond-waies" and fitted with a distinctive string rim. This type of bottle was popular in England until c. 1720, often coloured dark amethyst or yellowish-brown. Attributed to the Ravenscroft factory, last decade of the 17th century; 7¼in.

INTRODUCTION

Cobalt. Used since earliest times to produce a wide range of pale to dark blues.

Copper. Produces turquoise, green or red, depending upon furnace conditions. All of these shades were known to glass-makers of ancient Egypt.

Gold. Used from the 17th century onwards to produce a ruby red.

Iron. Present naturally in most glass-making ingredients and if left untreated (i.e. no decolourising agent added to neutralise its presence) a green or brown tone results. If added deliberately to the·batch in sufficient quantity, a deep emerald green is created, and if combined with other metal oxides such as manganese or antimony, a range of yellows, ambers, browns and blacks can be produced.

Manganese. Employed by Egyptian and Roman glass-makers to create amethyst or purple and also used during the mediaeval period to create a rose-pink shade.

Silver. If used as a sulphide a deep yellow stain is achieved; employed on stained glass windows, for example, during the mediaeval period.

Tin. Used as an oxide to create opaque white (and opacity in other colours).

Since the 19th century the following have also been used as colouring agents:

Chromium. A yellow-green.

Nickel. Violet in potash-glass and yellow in soda-glass.

Selenium. Pink in soda-glass and amber in lead-glass. If combined with cadmium sulphide, a red "sealing wax" shade is produced.

Titanium. A yellow-brown.

Uranium. A fluorescent greenish-yellow (see also Vaseline, p. 220).

Many of the above have also been employed as decolourising agents, to neutralise the effects of any impurities present in the natural glass-making ingredients. For example, antimony was employed during the 2nd to 4th centuries AD to render glass colourless; thereafter manganese was used with greater frequency. Cobalt was also used as a decolourising agent during the late 18th century, and more recently selenium has been used for the same purpose.

HOW GLASS IS DECORATED

Apart from the colouring of glass, which is a form of decoration in itself, numerous other methods of ornamentation have been developed. These can be grouped broadly into four categories: the application of hot glass by marvering or trailing threads onto the surface of the vessel, or by fusing glass blobs and other shapes to the object;

Carafe in the *vetro a fili* style, composed of alternate white and blue swirling threads embedded in the clear glass. Clichy, about 1850.

INTRODUCTION

painting the surface by enamelling, gilding and cold-painting; incising the surface by cutting, engraving, etching or sand-blasting; and miscellaneous techniques (which do not fit easily into any of the above) such as splintering the surface of the vessel, as in "ice glass". Each method of ornamentation is described below in the context of the above-mentioned categories and with reference to those countries or craftsmen who became famous for their mastery of its execution (for further details, cross-reference should be made to the pages on different glass-making centres).

Adding glass to glass
This would appear to be the most obvious method of decorating glass, and one of the oldest, as the necessary materials are already at the disposal of the glass-maker whose task it is, simply, to apply and fuse glass to the body of the newly formed vessel. The scope for decorating glass in this manner is enormous.

Combed threads. This method was adopted by the glass-makers of ancient Egypt and appears commonly on small core-formed vessels. Threads of hot glass, usually of contrasting colour, were wound around the body of the piece and then "combed" or dragged across the surface by use of a pointed tool to create the desired wavy or zig-zag effect. The object was then marvered so that the exterior wall of the vessel was made even and smooth. The technique was later adopted by Roman glass-makers and featured also on the glass of the Middle East, Venice, Spain and England.

Trailed threads. This method differs from the above in that after the threads of softened glass were trailed onto the surface, the object was then re-heated to fuse the decoration *in relief*. There was no subsequent marvering. The technique was used by Roman glass-makers and appeared in most exaggerated form with the so-called "snake trailing", characterised by the extravagant looping of threads. Later, free-standing trails were employed to great effect on the stems of Venetian (and *façon de Venise*) drinking glasses, and in southern Spain glass-makers adorned domestic wares with threads placed haphazardly across the surface. In England, Ravenscroft's lead glass was frequently decorated with threads "nipt-diamond-waies", so-called as the trails were pincered to form diamond patterns.

Marvered-in blobs. This method is similar to that of combing threads; small fragments of glass, usually of contrasting colours, were marvered-in to the surface of the object, creating a blotchy, pebbled effect. The technique was exploited by Roman glass-makers, and later by French

Roman flask of pale greenish glass, decorated over the surface with undulating snake-thread trailing in opaque yellow. 2nd century AD; 3in.

Vase of white opal glass with pincered side-handles, splashed decoratively over the surface in blue. Spanish, 18th century.

craftsmen during the 17th century. The English "Nailsea" style also made use of opaque white and coloured glass blobs as an alternative to combed decoration.

Applied blobs and other motifs. The process of applying glass blobs and other shapes to the vessel, and then consolidating them to the object by re-heating, has been practised without a break since Roman times. Claw beakers, with their protruding claw shapes, became a standard form of drinking vessel during the early mediaeval period, when other wares with free-standing blobs and prunts were also produced. From the 16th century, *Römers* were made throughout the Netherlands and Rhineland regions, frequently decorated with the aptly-named raspberry prunts, while Venetian vessels show applied prunts moulded with animal and human masks.

Painting the surface

This is usually the work of a specialist decorator whose purpose is to paint the glass as an artist would a canvas. The plain, clear or coloured glass surfaces can be embellished by enamelling, gilding or cold-painting to create a variety of monochrome or polychrome effects.

Enamelling. This ancient technique was practised as early

19

INTRODUCTION

as the 15th century BC and differs from cold-painting in that the colours are permanent, fused to the object by re-firing it in a muffle kiln. The enamel consists basically of three components: a finely powdered metallic colouring agent, a fluxing substance, and an oil or water base for easy working. Once the painted design is complete, the object is re-fired so that the colours develop and become fixed to the surface.The re-heating of the object must be controlled carefully. If the temperature of the kiln becomes too high, the piece may begin to melt and deform; furthermore, the enamel and glass surfaces must have similar contraction rates so that each remains intact during fusion.

Enamelled decoration does not occur frequently until the late Islamic period of the 13th and 14th centuries, when it was reserved for large mosque lamps and luxury glass objects. During the late 15th century, the Venetians enamelled clear or coloured wares, and from the mid-16th century onwards the technique was adopted in Germany, where it remained a highly pervasive form of ornamentation.
Cold-painting. This technique involves the painting of coloured' pigments onto the glass surface, with no subsequent firing. The colours employed are oil- or lacquer-based and do not require any additional heating to develop their tone or to fuse them to the surface. The disadvantage

Left Cold-painted and gilded dish mounted on a stemmed foot, depicting Judith and Holofernes and dated 1551. The painting has survived in unusually good condition, and is thought to be Swiss.

Right Two enamelled and gilded scent bottles of blue tinted glass, cut overall with facets (the left with shallow diamonds) underneath the richly painted designs. Fitted with gold screw caps and inner glass stoppers. London or south Staffordshire, c. 1765; 2¾in (right).

of using this method is that the decoration can be worn away or damaged easily, and many old pieces that have been cold-painted have lost their original designs. Cold-painting was frequently reserved for those wares which were too big to be placed in the muffle kiln, or for pieces too fragile to sustain a second firing. In addition, the technique was employed by amateur decorators who had no access to a kiln.

Gilding. Gold can be used as paint, powder or foil, and is applied to the surface or the underside of the glass to create a variety of effects.

Gilding by painting onto the surface of the object was frequently combined with enamelling (both subsequently fired at low temperatures and fused to the exterior), as on Islamic mosque lamps and late 15th-century Venetian commemorative wares. Occasionally, gilding appeared as the only decoration, as employed by several English decorators in the late 18th and 19th centuries, for example on the "Bristol blue" wares of Isaac and Lazarus Jacobs. Alternatively, the gold can be painted on the surface with no

One of a pair of covered preserve dishes, cut profusely with fine relief diamonds and surmounted by a mushroom-shaped finial. English, c.1815.

subsequent firing; this "cold-gilding" is similar in method to the cold-painting described above. Gold-leaf has been employed since later Roman times, when it was engraved with religious motifs and placed under a second protective layer of colourless glass. This *fondi d'oro* was revived in the 18th century in Germany, where *Zwischengoldgläser* (gold between glass) decoration appeared on glass tumblers and goblets. Gold in powdered form, or as a thin foil, could also be fused to the outside surface of the glass if mixed with an adhesive such as honey, and fired at low temperatures to achieve reasonable permanence.

Incising the surface
The surface of glass can be incised in numerous ways with the aid of hand tools, rotating wheels and, more recently, chemicals and machinery to produce a range of effects which vary in depth from a barely perceptible film to a three-dimensional sculptural quality. The success of each method depends upon the durability and flexibility of the metal, and the technical and artistic virtuosity of the craftsman, his sympathy with the material, precision in the execution of the design and inventiveness in its creation.

Cutting. Examples of cut glass survive from the 1st century BC and Roman glass decorators (called *diatretarii*) developed three methods for its manufacture. The first involved cutting into the surface with the aid of a rotating wheel or lathe to produce shallow depressions, grooves and facets, similar to the cutting of semi-precious stones and rock crystal. The second involved the use of the wheel and hand tools to cut into the outermost layer of cased glass so that the decoration appeared in relief against the underlying dark or contrasting coloured ground. The "Portland Vase" in the British Museum is the most famous example of this painstaking process. The third and most astonishing technique involved the grinding away of a solid block of glass by the processes of cutting and under-cutting, so that the exterior wall was made to stand out in high relief from the rest of the vessel, but remain connected to it by a series of small, barely perceptible struts. These are known as cage cups and demonstrate the immense skills of the Roman *diatretarii*.

A popular and pervasive style of cutting developed in England and Ireland during the 18th and 19th centuries which was made more attractive by virtue of its appearance on the soft lead glass which imparted to it an unequalled brilliance and sparkle. This method of cutting deeply into the surface of the object, using rotating wheels, is still employed today, usually in four stages: i) marking: the pattern to be cut is first drawn or painted (with a mixture of red lead and turpentine) onto the exterior wall of the vessel;

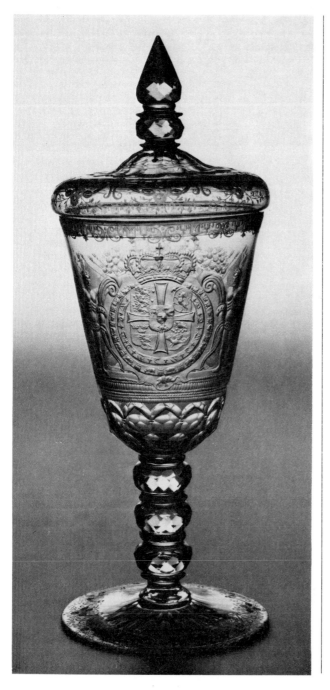

Large wheel-engraved goblet decorated with the arms of the King of Denmark, in the manner of the Saxon court glass engraver Johann Kiessling (d. 1744). It is recorded that the King of Denmark visited the Dresden court in c. 1720, and this goblet was probably made in his honour.

ii) roughing: the pattern is now roughly cut by the use of a revolving wheel of iron (or more recently, carborundum) about 18 inches in diameter, which is kept continually coated with fine wet sand acting as an abrasive; the object is held against the wheel-edge – either flat, convex or V-shaped depending upon the cut required – and moved so that the marked pattern is followed; iii) smoothing: to refine and perfect the roughly cut surface, a copper or sandstone wheel (similarly edged, as above) coated with fine emery or sand is used; iv) polishing: to achieve a high lustre, one of two methods is employed – a) polishing with a felt wheel, or wooden wheel coated with putty powder (or other fine abrasive) or b) for a lustrous sheen, dipping the object into a mixture of hydrofluoric and sulphuric acids, which attack the surface of the glass. The latter method is widely used today, being quick and inexpensive.

Surprisingly, only three types of incision can be made – flat, hollow or mitre (using a wheel with a flat, round or V-shaped edge respectively). Nevertheless, a variety of complex patterns can be created by combining these. Characteristic motifs (all straight-lined) include simple hollow or oval facet-cuts (called printies or thumbmarks) and a wide assortment of flutes, stars, hexagons, fans and diamonds. Cutting in curves can also be achieved, but this is a relatively difficult technique as it requires the craftsman to follow the decorative line while the object is at the wheel.

Engraving. This technique involves the cutting or scratching of the glass surface by means of a sharply pointed tool, or by using a rotating wheel. Basically, three types evolved.

Wheel-engraving, known since antiquity, is similar to the cutting technique described above with the exception that the wheel is small (varying in diameter from the size of a pin-head to about 4 inches) and made of copper. The vessel is pressed gently against the underside of the rotating wheel (operated by foot or, more recently, machine) which is fed continuously with an abrasive consisting of fine emery and oil. Engraved lines are formed easily on contact with the wheel, so flexibility and accuracy in working are essential (particularly as the oil makes visibility difficult). The technique became an important form of decoration in Germany and Bohemia during the 17th century and, like all forms of engraving, was best executed on a metal that was durable and thick.

Diamond-point engraving is executed with a pointed hand tool enclosing a diamond or other hard substance at the nib, which is scratched lightly into the surface of the object. The technique has been practised since Roman times, although it was not employed extensively until the late 16th century in northern Europe.

Stipple engraving with a diamond-point is similar

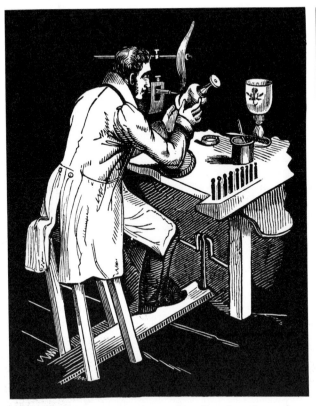

A glass engraver using a lathe operated by a foot treadle. Note the copper discs (right) of various diameters which, combined with emery moistened with oil, are used to engrave the glass. From F. Knapp *Chemical Technology*, Philadelphia, 1849.

to the above, but instead of scratching lines into the surface, the exterior is gently tapped to create numerous small dots which form the overall design. Dutch decorators developed this technique during the early 1700s.

Etching (sometimes called "acid engraving") is a relatively new form of glass decoration, not employed extensively before the 19th century. The technique involves the use of hydrofluoric acid (discovered in 1771) which eats into the walls of the glass, leaving behind a clear, frosted or pitted surface (depending upon the strength of the acid, and the length of the treatment). First, the object is covered with an acid-resistant substance such as wax or varnish. The required design is drawn into this coating with a pointed instrument. The hydrofluoric acid, usually mixed with potassium fluoride and water, is then applied to the object and attacks the exposed areas of glass where the wax has been removed. The glass is finally washed to reveal the etched surface design. Many French Art Nouveau designers, including Émile Gallé, employed this method of decoration during the late 19th century; it was also adopted in England for the commercial manufacture of cameo glass and for the application of mat patterns on clear glass.

Sand-blasting. This process was invented in 1870 by the American chemist Benjamin Tilghman, but has been employed only recently for the decoration of glass. The object is first covered with a protective mask which exposes parts of the underlying glass according to the required design, and the whole is then subjected to blasts of sand (or other abrasive such as powdered iron or flint) projected at high velocity from a special gun. The result is a finely pitted or greyish frosted effect which varies according to the type of abrasive used and the force at which it is expelled. The French designer René Lalique employed sand-blasting for decorative purposes and for the "R. Lalique" trademark.

Miscellaneous techniques

Pattern-moulding. A process employed commonly by Roman glass-makers (e.g. for the manufacture of Janus flasks), and later an important method of decoration in the U.S.A. and Europe. This relatively simple technique has the advantage of shaping and decorating objects at the same time, as the hot glass is blown into the patterned mould.

Ice glass. Characterised by a splintered surface effect, developed in Venice during the 16th century (see p. 58).

Pressed hemispherical bowl of opaque white glass, adorned with a panelled design of scrolling vines and daisies. The reeded interior has a decorative floral medallion at the centre. American, 19th century.

INTRODUCTION

Mosaic glass. Known since antiquity and used for wall plaques and vessels. The process involves the fusing together of numerous blobs of hot glass of contrasting colours, drawing them out into thin canes, and subsequently cutting them into small pieces. The next stage is to place the fragments onto a core, in the form of the required object, and covering the whole with a mould to keep them in place, to heat and fuse the pieces together. The mould is afterwards removed, and the mosaic surface smoothed and polished.

Millefiori glass. A variation of the above, but here the small coloured canes resemble a carpet of minute flowers. The technique was used in Roman times, and revived during the 16th century in Venice when the term *millefiori* ("a thousand flowers") was first employed.

Filigree glass. This style of decoration (the name means "thread-grained") developed in Venice by the early 16th century and is characterised by the use of opaque white

Rare pair of *millefiori* tazze, composed of brightly coloured and closely packed canes including silhouettes of shamrocks and Maltese crosses, each signed "B". Mounted on double-series opaque-twist stems, and *millefiori* feet. Baccarat; $3\frac{1}{2}$in.

and/or coloured threads of glass which appear in various straight, curved or twisted patterns *within* the metal. The method of making filigree glass is complex: the glass-blower gathers a small quantity of white or coloured glass onto the blow-pipe and marvers it to form a compact cylindrical mass, which is cooled. This piece is then dipped into clear molten glass, forming a second overlying layer, and the whole is marvered into the shape of a small cane, about 3 inches in diameter. The cane is re-heated and drawn out to a thin thread. Great quantities of threads were made in this manner, in various colour combinations, and 50 or more of these may be interlaced and fused together to form intricate filigree patterns.

Façon de Venise goblet of *vetro a retorti* style, mounted on a contemporary gilt-metal stem and foot. Antwerp, c. 1600.

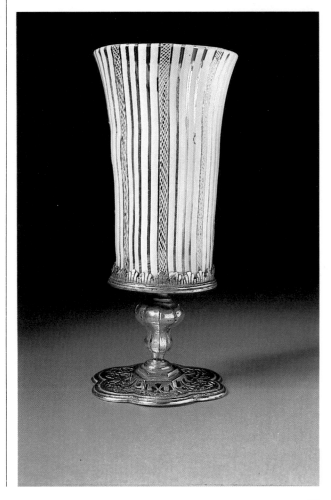

A SHORT HISTORY

ANCIENT EGYPT

Historians have suggested recently that the earliest manufacture of glass occurred in western Asia by about 3,000 BC, on the evidence of fragments which have been excavated in the region of Mesopotamia. Previously, research had indicated that glass was first made in Egypt, in the Nile delta, but this is considered now to be an outdated theory. Prior to 3,000 BC, Egyptian craftsmen were familiar with glaze techniques, and small objects of the period in stone, pottery and "faience" (ground quartz fused by an alkali and fired) have been discovered, covered with vitreous blue and green-tinted glazes. These beads, scarabs and amulets were the precursors of those in glass, and it was not until about 2,500–2,000 BC in Egypt that the latter was used as a principal material in its own right. During this early period of glass manufacture the same items continued to be produced, modelled on their stone and ceramic prototypes. Small amulets were made by pressing or pouring hot glass into stone moulds. Beads were created either by cutting small sections from heated glass rods, and decorating them by pressing threads into the surface, or by fusing different coloured layers of glass together, wrapping them around an iron wire to create zig-zag effects, and polishing to attain a smooth, continuous surface. Glass beads were as highly prized as gold and semi-precious stones, and were

Selection of core-formed vessels decorated with opaque coloured threads in festoons and spiral patterns. These small containers were used for aromatic oils and cosmetics. Egyptian, 14th–1st centuries BC.

pervasive objects of trade. Egyptian examples were exported widely throughout the ancient world.

Glass *vessels* do not appear in Egypt before c. 1,500 BC. The earliest dated examples (of which there are three, one in the British Museum) bear the cartouche of the pharaoh Tuthmosis III (1479–1425 BC), one of the most important rulers of the New Kingdom 18th Dynasty (1550–1307). It is thought that the Near Eastern conquests of Tuthmosis III led to the founding of a glass vessel industry, when the techniques were brought to Egypt by glass-makers of those regions. This would also account for the sudden appearance of glass vessels in Egypt, as there is little evidence of a transitional phase from the time of earlier bead-making.

Glass manufacture during the 18th Dynasty achieved high standards of technical and artistic accomplishment. The majority of wares – of small size, usually 4–8 inches high, and intended to hold perfumes, oils and cosmetics – catered for an exclusive market of wealthy patrons and nobility. Basically, five methods were used:

Molten glass fashioned on a core. This process was most commonly employed, although it required great skill. A clay, mud or straw core (often called a sand core, although recent evidence has suggested that sand was not used for this purpose) was formed on a metal rod, and shaped to resemble the desired object. This was then dipped several times into molten glass, or alternatively the hot glass was trailed around the core. When the walls of the vessel became thick, the object was marvered on a flat surface and details such as neck rims and handles could then be applied. Once the piece was annealed, the core was removed easily, leaving a rough, pitted interior. Numerous jugs, bottles and flasks were produced by this method, brightly coloured and decorated by zig-zag combing (see p. 18).

Sections of coloured glass rods fused to a core. This was used primarily for making dishes and bowls of mosaic glass (see also p. 28). Sections from monochrome and polychrome glass rods were built up on a core, and fused to produce mosaic effects, or alternatively the sections were placed in shaped moulds and fused. After cooling, surface imperfections could be removed by grinding.

Cutting from raw blocks of glass. This was done by chipping with a tool of greater hardness than glass (e.g. quartz or flint) as if sculpting from stone, a laborious method, seldom used before the 8th century BC.

Casting in moulds. Objects such as ornaments, inlays, small statuettes and, later, hollow ware were produced by either pressing in open moulds, or casting in two-piece moulds for modelling in the round – a technique derived from ceramic production.

A SHORT HISTORY

Egyptian blue glass stand, inscribed in hieroglyphics with a prayer and the cartouche of Amenhotep III (c. 1411–1375 BC). This piece is extremely rare, being one of only a handful of glass objects surviving from c. 1400 BC. It may have been used as the base for a small figurine; 2⅓in high.

Cire perdue or the "lost wax" method, a process whereby the article was modelled in wax and covered with clay. Once the wax had been melted and poured away, the gap could be re-filled with molten glass.

Favoured colours of the 18th Dynasty onwards were rich and opaque, in imitation of semi-precious stones, such as sky and dark blue (generally reserved for background areas), grey, yellow, white and occasionally orange, for decorative "trailing". Red, green and violet appeared with greater frequency later.

The production of bowls, urns and other small vessels continued in Egypt with little change until not long after 1,200 BC, when manufacture came to an abrupt halt. The industry did not resume until about 900 BC, after a long period of political and economic turmoil, although glass beads, seals and trinkets are found dating from that time.

During the 7th and 6th centuries BC, the manufacture of glass vessels once again became firmly established and a great diversity of forms, based on Greek ceramic prototypes, was now to appear commonly (these were exported widely). The *alabastron*, a cigar-shaped vessel with or without handles, was produced in Egypt and throughout Mediterranean and Middle East regions, as were the pear-shaped *amphora* (or *amphoriskos*, a smaller version), the *oenochoë* (jug) and the globular bottle known as an *aryballos* (for bath oils, suspended from the wrist by a cord). Core methods and decorative glass trailing were main-

tained, based on 18th Dynasty models, and objects continued to be of small size, used as containers for kohl (for outlining eyes) and other cosmetics, for oils and perfumes. Few innovations occurred during the next few centuries (although decorative "feather" patterns evolved, consisting of semicircular loops placed in vertical bands around the walls of the vessel) and by the 3rd century BC, there had been a general decline in standards, affecting both form and ornamentation. Carrying handles degenerated into stubs, and then disappeared completely, shapes became increasingly distorted and designs were applied with less precision.

When Alexander the Great founded Alexandria in 332 BC, the glass industry flourished again under the rule of the luxury-conscious Ptolemies (332–30 BC). Alexandria became one of the most important glass-making centres from Hellenistic times onwards (as did the Syrian coast), and although its cultural life reflected that of Greece, the achievements of the glass industry were due entirely to the efforts of Egyptian craftsmen who worked there. The wall plaques of mosaic glass, *millefiori* beads and bowls, brightly coloured vessels moulded in relief, and bangles and other forms of jewellery were greatly admired throughout the ancient world. The majority of these continued to be produced by the old methods, as Egyptian craftsmen were reluctant to learn the techniques of glass blowing (see next chapter), which they viewed as profane and ungodly. In 27 BC, Egypt was conquered by the Romans and from this period onwards, fine Alexandrian products were exported to Rome and throughout the empire.

Characteristic Egyptian vessel-types, all core-formed and adorned with brightly coloured trails. *Above* A round *aryballos. Bottom, left to right Amphoriskos* with bold "feather" patterning; cigar-shaped *alabastron* with small side handles; *oenochoë* with pinched-in lip and large vertical handle, set on a splayed foot; bottle in the shape of a palm-leaf column.

A SHORT HISTORY

The majority of examples found for purchase today – *alabastra, aryballoi* and *amphoriskoi* – are of relatively late manufacture, from after the 6th century BC. Many have survived intact due to the Egyptian custom of burying the dead amongst worldly goods, and as a result of the dry soil and arid climate of that region few pieces show signs of surface decay or iridescence.

ROMAN GLASS
The term "Roman glass" is used here in its broadest sense, to describe those objects which were made throughout the empire during the first four centuries of the Christian era – an area which included most of Europe, and extended in the Near East to places such as Syria, Palestine and Alexandria. It is important to realise that while some pieces can be attributed to specific localities (discussed below), the majority of examples are labelled simply "Roman" – a term indicative of age rather than origin.

Mould-blown jug in cobalt blue glass with olive green (weathered) handle, decorated in relief with symbols of athletic or religious significance placed in panels around the body. Sidonian, 1st century AD; 4in.

Fusiform "gold-band" *alabastron*, decorated overall with multi-coloured and gold wavy bands. Perhaps originally fitted with a separate rim and neck-piece. 1st century BC–1st century AD; $4\frac{3}{8}$in.

By the end of the 1st century BC, two important events had occurred which had a considerable impact on glass-making. The first was the invention of glass-blowing, possibly at Sidon, in Syria, which led to the inexpensive and efficient manufacture of glass objects, and the introduction of new forms (see How Glass Is Made, p. 10). The second was the founding of the Roman empire, and the subsequent spreading and infiltration of its culture, beliefs and ideas to all the provinces. The established glass industries of the East – particularly those at Alexandria and on the Syrian coast – exported their wares to Rome, the focal point of the empire, and from there they were brought to the colonies of Europe, where local workshops were shortly to be established.

During the 1st century AD (the early imperial period), glass manufacture in the East continued on a large scale in Syria, Palestine and at Alexandria. The productions of each region remained distinctive. Syrian glass-makers were among the first to employ the techniques of mould-blowing for domestic wares, a method by which the hot glass was suspended at one end of a blow-pipe and placed inside a hollow wood or clay mould, then blown into the pre-conceived shape. Numerous vessels (cups, flasks, bottles, etc.) have survived from this period, undoubtedly mass-produced as important articles of trade. Some examples were stamped or moulded with their maker's name and place of origin, and among the most prolific of Syrian glass-makers was the craftsman called Ennion, whose name appears on a variety of mould-blown jugs, cups and two-handled vases. Like many of his contemporaries, he soon transferred his workshops to the Italian peninsula to meet the increasing demands there for utilitarian glass wares. In contrast to the Syrian manufacture of simple mould-blown vessels, Alexandrian glass-makers continued to produce luxury objects modelled on pre-Roman prototypes and catering to the wealthy classes and nobility of Rome.

At the same time as the glass-makers of Syria and Egypt were exporting their wares, a steady stream of migrant craftsmen were leaving their homelands to settle in Italy and, later, other Roman colonies of the West. By AD 14, glass-houses were established in Rome by Egyptian and Syrian artisans. There soon followed a rapid spread of techniques, as craftsmen extended their activities from Italy into the provinces of Gaul (France), Germany and alpine regions by AD 50. By the end of the 1st century, glass factories in the Rhineland and at Cologne had become well known and were soon to rival those at Sidon and Alexandria; during the 2nd century workshops in Gaul and Belgium (and possibly in England) were also in production. In these areas, both mould-blown and free-blown domestic wares were manufactured in large numbers, showing great

A SHORT HISTORY

Left Two pillar-moulded bowls; *left* of marbled agate glass; *right* of amber, displaying iridescence and weathering. Note the distinctive vertical ribs which radiate upwards from the base. 1st century BC–1st century AD.

Below Mould-blown square bottle with applied "celery" handle, of a type produced commonly during the early Roman period.

similarity to those made in Italy and the Middle East. This widespread uniformity of style and decoration has caused great difficulty in distinguishing the local products of one area from those of the next, and while individual developments occurred (and can sometimes be traced) in specific localities, the majority of pieces cannot be ascribed easily to a place of manufacture.

The tremendous variety of glass wares produced throughout the Roman empire can be classified broadly into two major categories: firstly, items produced for ordinary domestic use, including bottles, sprinklers, jugs, flasks, beakers, goblets, vases, jars, etc. and, secondly, those created for a luxury market, intended for decorative use, religious purposes and ritualistic burials. The most important vessel-types from each group are outlined briefly below, with particular reference to those of artistic merit and to the techniques employed for their execution.

Household glass

Many early Roman domestic wares were coloured and somewhat severe in form, being straight and multi-sided (particularly when mould-blown, or "pillar-moulded" by working the vessel with pincers to form vertical struts), sometimes with thick ribbed handles called "celery" or "strap" handles. Later, shapes became increasingly elegant and fanciful, with a conscious play on the juxtaposition of forms and contrasting ornamentation (e.g. upward-curving handles and pervasive "snake-thread" decoration). Interesting and popular productions include the following:

Janus flasks, often coloured in monochrome green, blue or opaque white, and decorated with moulded masks in relief, usually on both sides of the body. Many of the heads were grotesquely and imprecisely fashioned. Numerous examples have been excavated in Syria and Palestine (where it is thought that the finest pieces were made) and in Gaul and Rhineland regions.

Right A flask with brilliant rainbow iridescence, displaying erratic snake-thread decoration. Roman, late 2nd–3rd century AD, $8\frac{1}{2}$in.

Below Opaque white Janus flasks, and hexagonal flask (*centre*) moulded in relief with flying birds placed in niches around the body. Roman, 1st–2nd century AD; average height 3in.

A SHORT HISTORY

Beakers, concave-sided, or mould-blown with bosses, a type of drinking vessel thought to be of Syrian origin, although specimens have also been excavated at Pompeii and in southern France. Examples are characterised by bosses which appear in rows, or at random, around the walls of the body – placed there to facilitate holding and possibly in imitation of round and polished cabochon jewels.

Victory cups, usually of cylindrical shape and mould-blown, with relief decoration consisting of laurels and inscriptions in celebration of a particular event. Examples have been excavated in Gaul and elsewhere in the West, many showing a maker's name on the base (e.g. that of Frontinus, a well-known craftsman who worked at Boulogne or Amiens about AD 300).

Circus cups, mould-blown vessels decorated with depictions, in relief, of chariot races and prize fights, produced in Gaul and elsewhere in the 1st and 2nd centuries.

Small perfume and toilet bottles (*unguentaria*) with polychrome surfaces, frequently decorated with applied threads trailed onto the surface in the old Egyptian tradition. The Romans, however, employed this technique with less accuracy, as in "snake-thread" trailing where strands of glass were looped and zig-zagged haphazardly across the whole of the exterior. Other designs were mottled; here small pieces of glass were marvered into the walls of the vessel to create a blotchy effect.

Storage vessels for holding oils and other liquids, or used as cinerary urns. Both coloured and colourless specimens were produced (the latter achieved by the addition of manganese as a decolouriser, from the 1st century onwards), often decorated with glass threads, or distinguished by cut linear bands and other indentations.

Coloured and colourless flasks and bottles, for pharmaceutical use, some examples stamped with the names of medicines which they were intended to hold.

Lenses, mirror fragments and window glass have also been discovered at Pompeii and elsewhere.

Large numbers of household wares have survived, many featuring brilliant iridescence on their surfaces. The iridescence results from the effects of burial. Chemical reactions with damp soil have caused a prismatic break-up of light, producing opalescent, rainbow colours which may appear evenly, or in flaky patches over the surface. In severe cases, however, the iridescence and associated changes can penetrate deeper, making the object very fragile.

Artistic glass

Glass objects which demonstrate immense technical and artistic accomplishment were made by master craftsmen in

Above Rare cage-cup or *vasa diatreta* of clear colourless glass, covered with an intricate network of pierced circular motifs. White flaking iridescence can be seen on the exterior and interior surfaces. Possibly made in the Rhineland, c. 300 AD; 4in high.

Above left Roman mould-blown circus cup, inscribed with a victory message and decorated in relief with a chariot and animals. Mid-1st century.

Below left The Portland Vase of coloured glass overlaid in opaque white, and carved with classical figures; 9¾in.

Rome, Alexandria and other important centres of the empire from the 1st century AD onwards. Indeed, the combined efforts of the glass-maker (i.e. moulders and blowers, called *vitrearii*) and the glass-decorator (i.e. cutters and engravers, called *diatretarii*) have, in some cases, never been surpassed. Outstanding types include:

Cameo glass, created by dipping a still hot, darkly coloured glass object (usually blue) into a crucible containing molten opaque white glass – a most difficult process due to the differing contracting rates of each layer as it cools. Once it all had cooled without breakage, the outer layer, the casing, could be carved to varying depths to create subtleties of shade, exposing the dark ground below according to the design. The most outstanding example of this technique is the "Portland Vase" in the British Museum, which is usually attributed to early Roman manufacture. (John Northwood and others made copies of it during the 19th century – see Later Artists and Decorative Styles, pp. 221, 223.)

"Cage" cups or *vasa diatreta*, consisting of bowls or cups with rounded sides, to which a complex network of pierced decorative motifs (either geometric or naturalistic in design) were attached by small, barely visible struts. This outer layer of ornamentation was not fused to the surface after carving, as was once believed, but the entire object created out of a solid block of glass by the very complex

39

process of under-cutting. It has been suggested that this latter method was executed under water to reduce the risks of breakage, but there is no proof of this theory. Pieces are rare and date from the 4th and 5th centuries, probably produced in Italy and in workshops at Cologne and Trier. An outstanding example of this technique is the "Lycurgus Cup" (in the British Museum) made during the 4th century, which is also prized for its dispersed colour effects ranging from an opaque green in reflected light to deep red in transmitted light. Other fine examples are in museum collections in Vienna, Budapest, Berlin, Munich, Venice and Milan.

"Gold sandwich glass" (or *fondi d'oro*), where a disc of glass was overlaid with gold leaf and engraved with a design. The gold was then covered with a final layer of glass to form a protected medallion, which was often placed at the bottom of a shallow dish or bowl. Several examples have been discovered in catacombs near Rome, dating from the 3rd or 4th century (although the technique was known earlier). These gold-leaf medallions were found embedded in the walls, broken away from the rest of the bowl and probably placed there by the family of the deceased as grave-markers. Many of the engraved subjects were of biblical content, depicting Christian and Jewish themes, although pagan subjects were also employed. Examples were also made in the Rhineland.

Vasa murrhina, glass vessels in imitation of striated hard-stones such as agate. The technique was well known in Alexandria from early times, and examples continued to be popular as luxury items during the 1st century.

Mosaic and **millefiori** wall plaques and bowls, the latter often edged with opaque white threads in twisted rope patterns. Examples were made in Alexandria and exported widely.

Enamelled and **cold-painted vessels:** both types are rare today, particularly the latter with its unfired colours which have largely disappeared through wear. Enamelling, however, was sometimes combined with gilding, as in the "Daphne Ewer" (Corning Museum, New York).

Other decorative techniques employed during Roman times included facet-cutting on bowls and cups, many exported from Syria and Egypt during the 1st and 2nd centuries; diamond-point engraving, usually reserved for colourless bowls during the 2nd century, depicting mythological scenes (it is doubtful, however, whether diamond-nibbed tools were used at this early stage); and wheel-engraving for simple ornamentation.

The fall of the western Roman empire in the early 5th century led to a dramatic decline in glass production, particularly of artistic and decorative wares. In the East,

The Lycurgus Cup, 4th century AD; $6\frac{1}{2}$ in high.

ROMAN GLASS, ISLAMIC GLASS

however, manufacture continued and flourished under Byzantine rule. (See Collecting, pp. 237–41 on present-day availability of Roman glass.)

ISLAMIC GLASS

By AD 350, political power had been transferred from Rome to Constantinople, where artistic glass manufacture continued, particularly in the form of mosaic wall decorations and window glass. There is little evidence, however, of a large glass-making industry, possibly as a result of its proximity to the well-established Syrian factories at Tyre and Sidon, where a wide range of wares continued to be produced in quantity. Indeed, it is possible that the glass objects which were manufactured in Constantinople during this early period were modelled on Syrian prototypes, and that many items for everyday use were imported from Syria, Palestine and Egypt.

During the 5th century, luxury and artistic glass was also made in Persia and Mesopotamia, where the practice of cutting glass in facets and geometric patterns developed, later to be incorporated into Islamic designs. These established factories continued to produce glass during the decline of the Roman empire, and provided the link in style and form between the classical designs of Greece and Rome and the Islamic work that was to follow. During the course of the 7th century, all of these Near Eastern countries (and also Palestine and other parts of North Africa) were conquered by Arab armies under the influence of Islam, and in 634, Damascus (in Syria) was established as the new Islamic capital. The glass productions of this early Islamic period (the Umayyad dynasty, 661–750) were based largely on Syrian prototypes (i.e. mould-blown and free-blown vessels for domestic use), with apparently little demand for artistic wares until the succeeding Abbasid dynasty (750–1258) and the founding of its capital at Baghdad, in Mesopotamia.

With the advent of the Abbasid rulers, the countries which formed the Islamic empire became firmly established as a single and self-contained entity. From the middle of the 8th century onwards, "Islamic" glass was produced to meet the demands of this newly formed nation, with a characteristic and distinctive style of glass object first appearing in Mesopotamia, where the influence of Persia was particularly pronounced. By the 9th century, both Baghdad and Basra were highly acclaimed glass-making centres, and numerous cut glass pieces from this period have survived, probably manufactured in response to the demands of the Caliph and his court. Recent excavations at Samarra, where the Abbasid rulers resided from 833 to 883, have unearthed large numbers of fragments which indicate the types of

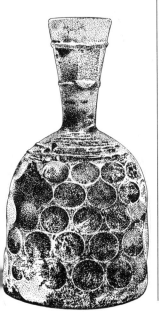

Below Persian flask cut around the neck and shoulder with panels and bands, and concavities below in a honeycomb pattern. 9th century AD.

A SHORT HISTORY

glass wares which were produced at this time. These include: a variety of *millefiori* and mosaic examples based on earlier Alexandrian styles (although distinct from the latter in the use of opaque yellow and other new colour combinations, and the presence of decorative dotted circles, which resemble eyes); various mould-blown objects decorated with applied and trailed threads, such as sprinkler bottles for perfume, and high-shouldered flagons with globular bodies and tall or short necks of distinctive oriental form; and cut glass fragments (see below).

Both innovative and well-established decorative styles and shapes were developed during the Islamic period. Many objects cannot be ascribed with certainty to a particular place of manufacture, or to a specific period of time. This is largely because many craftsmen travelled throughout the Islamic empire, and because various forms remained popular for centuries. The most distinctive Islamic styles (and shapes) are briefly outlined below.

Cut decoration. Glass centres of Mesopotamia were famous for this technique, also later practised in Persia during the 9th and 10th centuries. Examples include: i) facet-cut decoration, usually as concave oval shapes which occur over the body of, commonly, flasks and hemispherical bowls – creating a honeycomb effect; ii) linear-cut decoration, also on flasks and bowls, frequently appearing as incised foliage patterns which could be polished; iii) relief-cutting (ornamentation standing out in relief, the background having been ground down), perhaps in imitation of hardstone carvings in Persia and Mesopotamia, and the rock-crystal carving of Egypt during the Fatimid period. The earliest examples date from the 9th century, and were exported widely. Many were made of clear colourless glass in imitation of rock crystal; iv) cameo-cutting, a continuing tradition since Roman times. Fragments have been excavated at Samarra, and whole specimens (where colourless glass has been overlaid in green or blue) have been found in Persia and Egypt.

Applied decoration. Many of the techniques described in the previous chapters continued to be employed. Mould-blown patterning, pincered decoration and the application of glass threads, combed and marvered into the walls of the vessel, were all used to adorn domestic wares.

Lustre-painting. This technique is thought to have first appeared in Egypt during the early Islamic period, and is similar to that used on contemporary tin-glazed pottery. The decoration consisted of films of colour which were painted onto the body of the vessel, becoming lustrous when fired. Lustre-painting on glass was probably also employed in Syrian workshops.

Gilding and enamelling. These techniques were used

Above Colourless facet-cut bottle, with tapering neck and globular body, resting on a pad foot. The decorative frieze consists of seven circles with central bosses, linked by swagged lines and highlighted by fine iridescence. Islamic, probably 9th century; 5in.

Right Syrian dropper flask or *Omom*, the long neck tapering to a narrow mouth, covered with pitted iridescence. 13th–14th century.

A SHORT HISTORY

An enamelled mosque lamp.
Syrian, c. 1330–45; 12½in.

frequently together, and the Near East (particularly Syria) was famous for both during the 13th and 14th centuries. The best known examples of gilding and colourful enamelling are the mosque lamps, or lanterns, intended to hang from the ceilings of holy places and decorated with abstract patterns, ornate arabesques and quotations from the Koran. Various bowls, sprinklers and flasks of Syrian manufacture also employ this combined ornamentation. Syrian examples are normally classified into the following groups or areas: i) Damascus, where mosque lamps and domestic wares were made c.1250–1400; ii) Aleppo, where it is thought that the famous "Luck of Edenhall" beaker was made with its red, blue and white enamelled decoration consisting of foliage and geometric patterns. Now in the Victoria and Albert Museum, London, the beaker was brought to England by the Crusaders during the late 14th century – as were other specimens of Islamic glass, which was much prized in mediaeval Europe; iii) Raqqa (in Syria also) during the 12th and 13th centuries, believed to be the provenance of the well-known "Goblet of the Eight Priests" (now destroyed) and similar pieces at museums in Chartres and London (British Museum) which display strapwork decoration on a white dotted background; iv) "Syro-Frankish" wares, the work of Syrian glassmakers at a Frankish court during the second half of the 13th century. The "Aldrevandini Beaker" (in the British Museum), decorated with a pattern of Swabian coats-of-arms, painted leaves and inscriptions, is thought by some experts to be an example, although others think it is more probable that the piece was made in Venice, not earlier than the 14th century; v) "Chinese-Islamic" work, possibly created at Damascus and Aleppo from the late 13th century, and identified by the presence of *chinoiserie* motifs, often outlined in red, including cloud scrolls, lotus flowers, phoenixes, etc. This Chinese influence was the result of the Mongol conquests and of the founding of the Yüan (Mongol) dynasty in China (1280–1368) which encouraged the increase of trade with Syria and the Near East.

In 1400, Damascus was captured by the Mongol conqueror Tamerlane. Following his invasions of Persia (Iran), Iraq, Armenia, Syria and India, the glass industry declined. In Persia, manufacture was not revived until the reign of Shah Abbas the Great (1587–1629) when the city of Shiraz became an important centre for glass-making.

CHINESE GLASS

Glass manufacture in China did not commence before the 5th century AD, when it is thought that the techniques were brought by merchants from the West. However, it is certain that glass was known in China before this time, probably imported there from the provinces of the Roman empire and, in particular, from Alexandria. Recent excavations of tombs of the Han dynasty (206 BC – AD 220) and earlier have yielded various glass fragments including beads, many of which indicate a Roman origin. Other small funerary objects such as the *cicada* (which rested on the tongue of the deceased) and the *pi* (a disc-shaped item which symbolised heaven) have also been excavated. These glass ornaments, in imitation of those traditionally carved in jade and other hardstones, perhaps suggest that Chinese craftsmen were familiar with simple glass-making techniques during this early period; they were possibly made

45

A SHORT HISTORY

either by melting down the glass which was imported from the Near East (and other places) and then re-forming and designing pieces to suit their own tastes, or by creating them from raw materials (indeed, scientific tests have traced the presence of barium, which does not occur in contemporary glass of the West, or in later Chinese productions). It may be assumed that the techniques of melting and moulding glass continued, intermittently, from the Han dynasty onwards, although blowing methods do not appear to have been employed until much later.

The history of glass-making in China until the mid-17th century remains largely untraceable as a result of poor documentation, and the Chinese preference for ceramic wares. The production of glass did not come under official control until 1680, in the reign of the Emperor Kangxi (1662–1722), when a glass-factory was established at the imperial household in Peking. Initial production, thought to have been stimulated by the presence of European craftsmen, included various bowls, vases and other domestic objects. These *kuan liao*, or "imperial glass", were created by moulding and blowing processes (the latter used with greater frequency from this time onwards). Many

Peking glass vessels displaying a variety of decorative styles (some rare) including relief-carving, gilding and cold-painting. 18th-early 19th century; 5–9in high.

examples bear a striking resemblance to contemporary monochrome ceramic ware, and both porcelain and glass pieces lack reign marks, a practice temporarily suspended during the last quarter of the 17th century.

Kuan liao were thought to have been manufactured exclusively for imperial use, and consisted of plain monochrome glass (as above), cased glass in two or more coloured layers with cameo-cut decoration, and clear or opaque white glass painted with enamelled motifs. (All of these continued to be produced later, as discussed below.) Several examples show crizzling on their surfaces, a form of glass "sickness" where the walls of the vessel (interior and exterior) have deteriorated as a result of a surplus of alkali present in the glass composition – an occurrence which has plagued the initial productions of many new glass-houses, such as that of George Ravenscroft in England during the late 17th century (see p. 68). Crizzling usually takes the form of scaling and crazing, sometimes also accompanied

Pair of Peking turquoise blue vases with carved decoration in the form of stiff leaves and floral scrolls, 11in. The shape of the "imperial yellow" vase is derived from the ancient ritual bronze called a *Ku*. All Qianlong period (1736–95).

A SHORT HISTORY

by a bad odour and viscidity. Apart from its destructive nature, crizzling may also cause the colour and transparency of the glass to alter and such effects have, in the past, complicated the task of dating.

By the early 18th century, the new Emperor Yongzheng reintroduced the practice of adding reign marks to ceramic and glass wares, frequently engraved on the base of the latter. Eighteenth-century examples, still of domestic form (bowls, vases, jars, etc.), achieved high standards of accomplishment in their brilliance of colour – particularly evident in the "imperial yellow" shade, which symbolised prosperity – and meticulous carved decoration executed on the lapidary's wheel.

When in 1736 the Emperor Qianlong came to the throne (he ruled until 1795), the imperial factory at Peking was transferred to Poshan in the northern province of Shantung. What is commonly referred to as "Peking glass" (*qing liao*) was manufactured from here, and then exported to Peking, either in a finished state, or as raw blocks to be shaped and adorned by craftsmen of that city. By this time, the most important decorative techniques had been mastered, including under-cutting and chiselling. "Peking glass" can be classified broadly into four categories. Transparent and translucent pieces were usually moulded and decorated with relief-cut designs, and coloured green, amber, blue, red or amethyst. Opaque and semi-opaque wares were similarly coloured, but were often unadorned to resemble their ceramic counterparts; well-known shades include "imperial yellow", and a curious pastel rose known as "boudoir pink". The third group, of overlay or cased glass in two or more shades, is perhaps the best known, recalling the earlier and highly accomplished work of Roman glass cameo-carvers and incorporating wheel-cutting and engraving, a technique believed to have been rediscovered by the Chinese during the early 18th century. Finally, glass was made in imitation of jade, marble, lapis lazuli and other semi-precious stones – and also, to simulate fine porcelain. The latter, produced since the late 17th or early 18th centuries, was achieved by use of opaque white glass in imitation of hard paste porcelain, upon which enamelled colours were painted in decorative patterns, frequently in a *famille rose* palette. The studio of Guyuexuan in the first half of the 18th century produced numerous small vessels, such as snuff bottles, in this medium and examples were sometimes marked with this name.

Chinese glass-making continued during the 19th and 20th centuries (see Snuff Bottles, p. 199; Glass Pictures – Mirror paintings, p. 212), although the majority of later pieces may be distinguished by a general decline in standards.

CHINESE GLASS, MEDIAEVAL EUROPE

Left to right Translucent vase of bluish-green glass; opaque red marbled vase; covered pot decorated with multi-coloured single overlays, carved variously with stylised dragons and clouds. Chinese, 18th–19th century.

MEDIAEVAL EUROPE

The decline of the Roman empire had an adverse effect on glass-making in Europe. Here, the production of artistic glass vessels ceased (not to be revived for another thousand years, with the Renaissance) and domestic wares were characterised by a marked deterioration in form, decoration and quality of metal. During the 5th to 8th centuries, however, a few new and curious glass shapes emerged under Teutonic influence, and the mediaeval church was to provide stimulus to the art of making stained glass. The absence of artistic glass objects in the West was barely compensated by the appearance of examples of Middle Eastern and Islamic origin, brought to Europe by Crusaders and preserved in numerous cathedral treasuries, such as that of St. Mark's in Venice. Such pieces were highly regarded and their quality of workmanship contrasted greatly with the primitive techniques and crude forms which were adhered to by mediaeval glass-makers of the West.

During the Merovingian or Frankish period (5th–8th centuries) glass-houses in the Rhineland, France, Belgium and probably England produced simple mould-blown wares for utilitarian purposes. While small jars and bottles for ointments, perfumes and the storage of other liquids continued to be made, their manufacture was limited in favour of a range of drinking vessels which were most popular in northern European regions. All vessel types of this period, and later, demonstrate a marked decline in the quality of their metal, lacking the clarity of earlier Roman pieces. Most examples are of green, brown or grey tone, due to chemical imperfections in the selected ingredients (not as a result of a conscious effort to achieve these tinges) and pieces frequently show the presence of bubbles and striations. Colours, on the whole, are considered to be of poor quality, showing little variation in shade (although amber and green-blue were sometimes employed) and marked by impurities of tone. Vessels which demonstrate these characteristics have been excavated throughout Europe – particularly in Germany, the Rhineland and the Netherlands, where the pagan practices of burying the deceased with worldly goods continued to be employed as late as the 10th and 11th centuries.

The use of decorative patterns by mediaeval European glass-makers was also restricted. The majority of examples demonstrate the continuing Roman traditions of simple mould-blown patterning, snake-thread trailing and other applied motifs. However, surface ornamentation which consisted of enamelling, cold-painting, cutting and other techniques which necessitated the use of hand tools were all forgotten or ignored.

Various woodland regions of Europe became centres for glass-making at this time. In the Rhineland, *Waldglas* ("forest glass") was entirely dependent upon the use of beech and other forms of wood-ash for the essential alkali which was needed to make glass. In France, the manu-facture of *verre de fougère* employed fern or bracken for this purpose, so that the end-products of each region were of marked similarity with regard to their composition and appearance. Forest glass-houses existed not only in

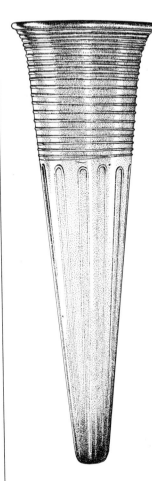

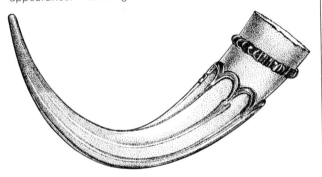

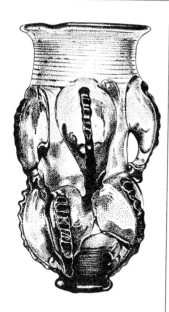

Germany and France, but also in Bohemia, in areas of modern Belgium and the southern Netherlands, and in the Weald region of southern England. The identification of local types from these areas is difficult – a result of the absence of documentary evidence, the frequent moving of glass-houses as the supply of raw materials became depleted, and the uniformity of styles. It is important to realise that pieces excavated from one area were not necessarily manufactured there.

Briefly outlined below are the most commonly encountered glass vessels which have been excavated from regions throughout Europe. Many of these are discussed in greater detail in those pages which are devoted to specific types of object.

Drinking vessels. Particular types developed as early as the 5th century in the Rhineland and other northern regions. The majority are of green-tinted glass, are thick-walled, mould-blown and characterised by the absence of handles, foot and base. Many show trailed or other applied decoration in the form of threads, blobs and prunts. Cone-beakers and drinking horns were commonly produced, as were many simple tumblers and the well-known claw beakers or *Rüsselbecher* with their characteristic "claws", resembling elephants' trunks, which protruded from the exterior surface (see Beakers, pp. 100–102).

Above A claw beaker or *Rüsselbecher*, German, 5th–6th century; 8in.

Above left Cone beaker decorated with applied spiral trails in horizontal and vertical patterns; Frankish, 5th–6th century; 10in.

Left A glass drinking horn, Saxon, 5th–6th century; 13in from tip to rim.

Right Mediaeval beaker of finely seeded (bubbled) pale greenish glass, decorated with applied prunts between encircling spiral trails. Note the kick base. 14th century; 3⅔in.

A SHORT HISTORY

Left Warzenbecher of pale greenish colour, mould-blown with projecting nodules around the sides, and applied blue glass trail on the rim. *Right Krautstrunk* (cabbage-stalk) of bluish-green *Waldglas*, having a flared convex rim and double row of applied prunts. Both German, 15th century; average height 2⅓in.

Other domestic wares. These included bowls, vases and bottles, of which relatively few examples have survived largely as a result of the general decline in pagan tomb burials as Christian doctrines forbade the use of funerary objects. Bottles, bowls and vases were characteristically thick-walled and of green-tinted metal, often decorated with applied threads in simple looped patterns. Mediaeval glass-makers were also interested in the imitation of semi-precious stones, as is evident in several glass "recipes" which were recorded during the 9th and 10th centuries. However, it is doubtful whether their attempts to simulate gemstones were successful, and the importing of pieces of emerald- and sapphire-coloured glass from the Middle East continued. One famous example is the so-called "Sacre Catino" bowl of emerald colour, probably of Egyptian manufacture, which was brought to the Cathedral of S. Lorenzo at Genoa by Crusaders during the early 12th century. Several legends have been connected with this bowl – at different times, it was thought to represent the Holy Grail, and the dish upon which the head of St. John the Baptist was carried.

Ecclesiastical glass. Few glass vessels were produced for the church, and the use of glass was forbidden for ritualistic purposes due to its fragility and "poor quality". Some glass chalices have been excavated. The use of glass for windows and wall mosaics, however, was encouraged by the church as early as the 6th century, and by the 12th stained glass was manufactured widely throughout northwest Europe, particularly in France at glass centres in Lorraine and Normandy. It is likely that glass was exported from here to places such as England and Scandinavia (see also Stained

Glass, pp. 207–9), although it is documented that window glass was made during the 13th century in England at the factory of Laurence Vitrearius. Records tell of the constructing of clear and coloured glass windows for Henry III's Chapel at Westminster Abbey by Laurence Vitrearius in 1240, and similar commissions for the church continued in England and Ireland from this period onwards.

VENICE

It is recorded that a glass industry existed in Venice by the late 10th century, although very little is known about it due to the lack of both documentary evidence and original pieces. Coloured glass fragments for mosaics, recently excavated at the nearby island of Torcello, indicate that there may have been a glass-house there as early as the 7th century, and it is likely that Venice was also involved at this time in the manufacture of small vessels and beads in the Alexandrian style. The geographical position of Venice was such that good trading links had been maintained with the East, from where glass was exported to Venice and probably copied there "à la façon de Syrie". It was not until the 13th century that the glass industry in Venice became fully established, and the late 15th that easily recognisable styles emerged which enable pieces to be identified accurately.

Early mediaeval stained glass panel depicting The Annunciation, closely related in style to contemporary middle Byzantine painting. Probably from Torcello, c. 1200.

A SHORT HISTORY

Venetian glass is known to have been exported to northern Europe from the 15th century onwards, and from the time of the Renaissance their glass was in great demand at royal courts and by wealthy patrons. There were several reasons for the dramatic success of the industry, among them the strong geographical position of Venice, the decline in eastern glass manufacture with the fall of Constantinople in 1204 (and later in 1453, when captured by the Turks), the ensuing migration of eastern glass workers and techniques to Venice, which now succeeded to the role of world centre for glass-making, and the availability of the raw materials which were essential for its production. In addition, there were strict regulations enforced by the *Capitolare*, an agreement between the new glass-makers' guild and the Republic first drawn up in 1271, which forbade the migration of Venetian craftsmen and the exporting of their materials and techniques. This was to ensure that their methods remained secret and their achievements unsurpassed and, curiously, such rules were enforced for centuries thereafter until the guilds were finally disbanded in the early 19th century. However, penalties of imprisonment and even death could not prevent numerous Venetian glass-makers from travelling elsewhere, and this eventually led to the development of *façon de Venise* techniques throughout Europe.

In 1292, due to fears of fire spreading from the furnaces, the glass industry was removed from the highly populated city to the nearby island of Murano, some 3 miles away. Thus, from about 1300 to the present day, all "Venetian" glass has been made at glass-works in Murano. Initial production there included the making of beads – small ones by the *margaritai* and large and hollow ones by the *perlai* – lenses for spectacles (by the *cristallai*) and small pieces of pane glass called *rui*. By the late 15th century and the Renaissance, glass beakers, bottles and dishes were also produced.

The manufacture of fine quality and artistic glass wares commenced shortly after 1450, stimulated by Renaissance ideals. Most notable were the large armorial flasks and covered cups, and the richly coloured marriage or betrothal beakers, called *coppe nuziale*, with gilded and enamelled decoration consisting of medallion portraits and processional scenes. The famous wedding cup known as the "Barovier Cup" (in the Museo Vetrario, Murano), of dark blue glass, is decorated in this exuberant manner. (Now assigned to a date of about 1470, it was previously wrongly associated with the work of the pioneer glass-maker Angelo Barovier, who died shortly before this time.) Enamelling and gilding were popular during the second half of the 15th century. Ornate pictorial scenes soon gave way to simple

Venetian "betrothal" goblet, gilded and enamelled with two portrait medallions of a man and woman (probably the bride and groom), cupids and the motto 'AMOR. VOL. FEE' (Love Requires Faith). Late 15th century.

geometric patterns. Favoured motifs included fish-scale designs (also found on contemporary maiolica), and enamelled dots which resemble gemstones. Richly coloured glass was greatly in demand, notably bright blue, green, purple and turquoise (such as the well known opaque blue "Fairfax Cup" made in Murano about 1480, in the Victoria and Albert Museum, London), appearing as single colours, and often adorned with gilding and enamelling. By the early 16th century, however, the popularity of coloured glass had declined in favour of the excellent *cristallo*. Named after the rock crystal which it closely resembled, *cristallo* was a clear glass which was almost colourless, marked by a pale yellowish or brownish tinge, and was produced with the aid of manganese, employed as a decolourising agent. By the mid-16th century, *cristallo* was of an unsurpassed quality, surprisingly light and thin, the metal easily manipulated when blown and decorated. Like all glass of such a soda-lime variety, *cristallo* was highly plastic, lending itself well to elongation and fanciful decoration. These ductile qualities were fully exploited by Venetian craftsmen. *Cristallo* wares were frequently adorned with applied threads of bright blue, their forms manipulated by pulling the glass with pincers and tongs, as indicated frequently by the intricate stems of drinking glasses. Such elaborate decoration made Venetian *cristallo* famous throughout Europe.

Briefly outlined below are six categories of Venetian glass manufactured from the Renaissance period onwards. Many of the decorative techniques employed in their production are discussed more fully in "How Glass Is Decorated", pp. 16–29).

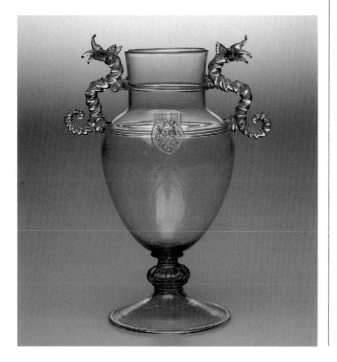

Venetian *cristallo* vase mounted on a ribbed knop and foot, with twisted handles in the form of dragons. Adorned with applied drops of blue glass and a moulded lion's mask (with traces of gilding) on the encircling bands of the body. 16th century; 11in.

Right A Venetian *cristallo tazza*, gilded and enamelled in a dotted scale pattern, with elaborate floral scrolls on the foot. About 1500.

Below Venetian *cristallo* candlestick of fanciful design, adorned with opaque blue and yellow threads forming a central floral medallion. 17th century; 10in.

Right A Venetian *cristallo tazza*, gilded and enamelled in a dotted scale pattern, with elaborate floral scrolls on the foot. About 1500.

Below Venetian *cristallo* candlestick of fanciful design, adorned with opaque blue and yellow threads forming a central floral medallion. 17th century; 10in.

Colourless, transparent wares (cristallo) and glass of single colours, including those mentioned previously and also amber, red, yellow and opal white. Numerous recipes for making coloured glass were published in Florence in 1612, in Antonio Neri's book *L'Arte Vetraria*. Examples were free- and mould-blown, and characteristically decorated with threads of coloured glass, in fanciful shapes.

Gilded and enamelled glass. The two techniques usually appeared together on clear and coloured wares, chiefly large bowls, *tazze* and goblets (the majority of drinking glasses were ill-suited to this decoration, being fragile and easily distorted). Sixteenth-century examples show elegance and refinement in their enamelled painting and commonly illustrate motifs such as floral scrolls, dotted patterns, armorial emblems and the lion of St. Mark.

Cold-painting (i.e. unfired colours) was also used, particularly during the early 18th century. Few fine pieces survive, however, due to the decorative surfaces being easily worn.

Engraving was seldom employed in Venice, again due to the thinness of the glass, although diamond-point engraving was fashionable for a brief time during the mid-16th century (and was very popular elsewhere in Europe).

A SHORT HISTORY

Ice glass (vetro a ghiaccio), an interesting 16th-century technique (and employed thereafter) where a hot glass bubble was plunged into cold water and then immediately reheated and blown to create a frozen or crackled ice appearance. Alternatively, the hot glass was rolled in finely splintered glass which, embedded in the surface, produced a similar effect.

Glass in imitation of semi-precious stones, hardstones, and porcelain. Techniques to simulate jasper, onyx, agate and chalcedony had been employed by Egyptian and Roman glass-makers, and were revived in Venice from the 15th century onwards. Aventurine glass was also manufactured, in imitation of aventurine quartz with its flecks of mica, by the addition of metallic copper to the glass. Chinese porcelain, which was much admired in Europe, was imitated by the use of opaque white glass (called *lattimo,* from *latte* meaning milk) which could then be painted. Glass imitations of porcelain were popular from about 1580 onwards, often being referred to as *porcellana contrafatta* ("counterfeit porcelain").

Millefiori and mosaic wares (also derived from Roman techniques) were produced from the 15th century onwards (see pp. 28 and 40).

Filigrana or **vetro filigranato** glass (literally, "thread-grained") was produced in Murano from the early 16th century onwards and was possibly inspired by Roman rope-twist patterns, as found on the rims of bowls. This technique made use of opaque white threads (called *latticino* or *latticinio*) and coloured threads in reds, blues and yellows,

Venetian filigree styles. *Above left: vetro a fili,* composed of broad bands. *Above right: vetro a reticello,* consisting of criss-crossed threads enclosing small air bubbles. *Below:* two examples of *vetro a retorti,* combining delicate lacy patterns.

Opalescent bowl from the Miotti glasshouse, enamelled in bright colours with flowers beneath a yellow stylised border. The interior is decorated with a goldfinch perched amongst wild strawberries. Venice, c. 1725–50; $2\frac{1}{4}$in high.

sometimes combined with white. Various types of *filigrana* were developed including: *vetro a fila*, where threads were placed in parallel lines, occurring in straight and spiral patterns; *vetro a reticello*, where threads were criss-crossed, and made to capture small air bubbles which were trapped between each "empty" space; and *vetro a retorti*, where threads were twisted, sometimes into lacy designs (*vetro di trina*) appearing in either simple or complex patterns. Each type could be used alone or in combination, and numerous variations evolved. (See the line drawings.)

These decorative styles, and the important production of mirror glass and chandeliers, continued with little interruption until the 18th century, when the Venetian glass industry declined. With the increased popularity of cut and engraved glass at this time, as produced successfully by Bohemian and German craftsmen, the Venetian industry lost much of its impact as it was unable to imitate this ornamentation on the delicate *cristallo* wares. However, during the mid-19th century, many Renaissance glass styles were revived, and today innovative wares are being produced at Murano by firms such as Venini and Barovier, the latter descended from the famous 15th-century Barovier family.

A SHORT HISTORY

GERMANY AND BOHEMIA (INCLUDING AUSTRIA)

Waldglas traditions (see Mediaeval Europe, p. 50) continued in forest regions of Germany during the 15th century, at the time of the artistic glass productions of Venice. The characteristic and curious vessel-types of this period and later, almost exclusively related to drinking, include: the *Maigelein*, a simple drinking cup with a high projected "kick" in the base, usually mould-blown; the *Römer*, a popular and pervasive form of drinking glass for Rhenish white wines, made in Germany and elsewhere; the *Kuttrolf* or *Angster*, a curiously shaped vessel used to hold spirits, characterised by small tubular sections in the neck or body for slow pouring or dripping; the *Stangenglas*, a tall cylindrical beaker; the *Passglas*, similar to the *Stangenglas* but with applied and notched threads around the body, used for communal drinking. Other variations of these tall glasses included the *Willkomm*, a glass offered to welcome guests; the *Nuppenbecher*; the *Warzenbecher*; and the *Krautstrunk* or "cabbage-stem" glass. (See also Beakers, pp. 100–102.) Many of these vessels were decorated with prunts, which were styled variously – drawn out to a fine point, stamped with patterns, spiked and curled downwards (recalling earlier claw beakers), or left simply as round blobs in relief. Prunts were sometimes combined with decoration such as enamelling on the same piece, but during the 16th century these motifs became less pervasive with the adoption of other important and refined forms of ornamentation.

Above Reichsadlerhumpen, enamelled and gilded with the conventional motifs of the double-headed crowned eagle of the Holy Roman Empire. German or Bohemian, dated 1614; 13¼in.

Left Common German vessels of the 16th and 17th centuries, for drinking and serving liquids. *Left to right* Kuttrolf with twisting tubes at the neck for slow pouring; Willkommhumpen, a drinking glass for welcoming visitors, decorated with portraits and greetings inscriptions; Nuppenbecher decorated with applied drops of glass; Passglas with enamel decoration and encircling bands, used for communal drinking; Stangenglas decorated with a coat-of-arms.

Façon de Venise

As mentioned in the previous chapter, the appearance of Italian craftsmen in Germany, Bohemia and Austria during the 16th century encouraged these countries to adopt the styles and forms made popular by the successful Venetian glass industry. Numerous factories were founded during the early part of the 16th century to produce pieces *à la façon de Venise*, at Hall (in the Tyrol, near Innsbruck), Nuremberg, Landshut, Munich, and elsewhere. Cologne and Vienna had joined these by the late 17th century. *Façon de Venise* wares of these northern countries are often difficult to distinguish from genuine Venetian or Italian products and as one historian commented "nothing is more exasperating than attempting to distinguish Venetian glass from so-called glass *à la façon de Venise ...*" (*German Enamelled Glass*, by Axel von Saldern; see Bibliography). In many cases, a definitive attribution is not possible.

Decorative techniques

Enamelling was initially inspired by Venetian examples, and was immensely popular in Germany and Bohemia from the mid-16th century onwards. The problems of identification mentioned above occur in many enamelled pieces of the Renaissance period, but German specimens, unlike their Venetian counterparts, were often dated. Enamelling in bright colours was most commonly reserved for the *Stangengläser, Walzenhumpen* (tall cylindrical vessels often decorated with armorial motifs), *Humpen* and beakers, with decorative patterns that invariably included coats-of-arms, and distinctive gilded bands of circles, stars and rosettes placed below the rim. It is thought that enamelling was first practised in the Bavarian forests, although other important centres emerged. Regional styles developed, but it is often difficult to determine a place of origin. A wide range of subjects was employed, including armorial and biblical themes, portraits, hunting scenes, landscapes, guild processions, etc. – occasionally accompanied by inscriptions.

During the 17th century, a new and important style of enamelling emerged in Nuremberg with black as the predominant pigment, sometimes accompanied by hints of red and gold, called *Schwarzlot*. In this technique, introduced by Johann Schaper (1621–70), decorative patterns were scratched into the black enamelled sections with a pointed instrument. Other transparent enamels were developed in the 17th century, in contrast to the heavy, opaque shades used earlier. Enamelling *en grisaille* (in grey, in imitation of relief sculpture) was sometimes combined with *Schwarzlot*, notably by Schaper and by Daniel Preissler of Silesia.

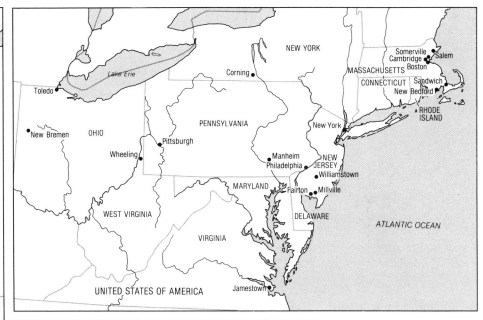

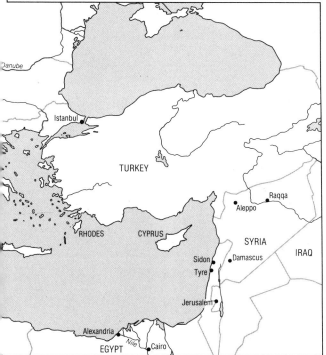

Principal glass-making centres of Europe and the United States, from early times to about 1900.

A SHORT HISTORY

Cold-painting (or *Kalte Malerei*) was also inspired by Venetian examples, using oil or lacquer-based pigments which were painted onto the surface, with no subsequent firing. The technique was employed throughout Germany from the 16th century onwards. Sometimes, the designs were painted on the interior walls of the vessels, or were covered by glass, varnish or foil to protect the work from wear and damage. Alternatively, the painting was executed on a gold or silver-foil ground. Cold-painting was also combined with gilding and with diamond-point engraving, particularly at Hall.

Far left Ruby glass tankard of baluster form, engraved with Cupid holding a heart and inscribed "Un Seul me Suffit". Silver mounts, Nuremberg or S. German, c. 1680–90; 5½in.

Left, above Clear glass goblet and cover featuring opaque red twists in the faceted knopped stem and finial, and engraved with swirling foliage. Bohemian, c. 1740; 11in.

Above Milchglas decanter and stopper, enamelled and gilded with an elaborate coat-of-arms and surmounted by the arms of the eight electors and Holy Roman Empire. The sides are decorated with bands of flowers. German, c. 1740; 10in.

Left Zwischengoldglas, decorated with a figural scene and red medallion at the base. Silesian, c. 1770.

Wheel- and diamond-point engraving developed in Germany to a high degree from the second half of the 16th century onwards. Early exponents of these techniques included Caspar Lehmann (1570–1622) who was appointed "Court Lapidary" to Emperor Rudolf II at Prague, and his pupil Georg Schwanhardt of Nuremberg (1601–67) who combined wheel- and diamond-point engraving in a single piece. By the last decades of the 17th century, both methods had become increasingly popular due to the introduction in Bohemia of a new and stable "metal", which was much better suited to cutting. This less fragile glass was produced by the use of potash (as opposed to the soda used by the Venetians for *cristallo*), and was given greater stability by the addition of chalk. By the 1680s, Friedrich Winter and his brother Martin were important exponents of engraving techniques on the new glass, which allowed for *Hochschnitt* (wheel-engraving in high relief) and *Tiefschnitt* (cutting deeply into the surface in *intaglio*). These were occasionally used together on a single piece, and several outstanding examples were produced during the late 17th and early 18th century.

Coloured glass was popular in northern countries, particularly the ruby-red shade which was developed by the glass chemist Johann Kunckel during the last quarter of the 17th century, by the use of gold chloride (described in his book *Ars vitraria experimentalis* or *Vollständige Glasmacherkunst* – "The Complete Art of Glassmaking" – published in 1679). Blue, green and opaque white (*Milchglas*, made in imitation of porcelain) were in common use from the 18th century onwards. Later, during the early 1800s, new colours were developed in Bohemia, including Hyalith (which was produced in sealing-wax red, or black) and Lithyalin glass, developed by Friedrich Egermann to imitate semi-precious stones. Various hues of yellow were also created by use of uranium (see Vaseline, p. 220).

Gold decoration was used in various forms, such as the well known *Zwichengoldgläser* ("gold between glass") where two drinking glasses were fitted closely together, one enclosing the other, with engraved decoration on gold or silver in between. Many fine examples were made in Bohemia c. 1730–55, inspired by Roman work (see p. 40).

Many of these decorative and traditional techniques continued to be employed, particularly in Bohemia, during the 19th and 20th centuries while at the same time other styles of ornamentation were also encouraged in keeping with the vogue for new colour effects. Many of these are described in Later Artists and Decorative Styles (pp. 214–35).

A SHORT HISTORY

ENGLISH GLASS

Glass-making in England was practised continuously from mediaeval times. Important developments were to occur, but the production of ordinary vessels for everyday use was little affected by the technical achievements of the industry. The various categories of manufacture are outlined briefly below, although specific vessel-types and the evolution of their forms are discussed separately, in the chapters devoted to those objects.

As in most of Europe during the mediaeval period, glass-making in England was carried out in woodland regions, particularly in the Weald of Kent, Surrey and Sussex. During the 13th century, craftsmen from Normandy settled in this area, such as the family of Laurence Vitrearius, who established a glass-works near Chiddingfold, in Surrey, before 1240. Production consisted chiefly of window glass-making for churches, although simple domestic vessels of green potash glass were also manufactured from the 12th century onwards, similar to the *Waldglas* of Germany and the *verre de fougère* of France (see Mediaeval Europe, pp. 49–53). By the 14th and 15th centuries, other centres of window glass-making existed at Oxford, Colchester, York and Gloucester. Although little is known of the industry during this time, it is likely that the demand was partly met by importing pieces from abroad.

It was not until the mid-16th century that the glass industry in England received its first important stimulus with the introduction of Venetian styles. In 1550, eight glass-makers from Murano were brought to London at the request of Edward VI, to teach the art of Venetian glass-making, but they stayed only a short time due to the strict regulations of the *Capitolare* (see p. 54). However, their departure was soon followed by the arrival in 1567 of Jean Carré, of Arras and Antwerp, who was permitted to manufacture both window glass and glass vessels *à la façon de Venise*. Carré also introduced into England window glass-making families from Lorraine, who initially settled in the Weald and competed with English craftsmen of that region, and by the last quarter of the 16th century had established new factories in Hampshire, Gloucestershire and north Staffordshire. Excavations in these areas have revealed thick green glass fragments and drinking vessels which suggest that common glass wares continued to be manufactured despite the influence of Venetian styles.

Carré's glass-house was set up in London at the abandoned monastery known as the Crutched Friars, near the Tower of London, and after his death production continued under the Italian Giacomo Verzelini (1522–1606). The factory was soon destroyed by fire and re-established at Broad Street, where Verzelini was granted

Goblet of soda glass mounted on a large melon-shaped knop and foot, by Giacomo Verzelini. The diamond-point engraving, depicting a stag, unicorn and hounds, is probably the work of Anthony de Lysle. Dated 1578; 8½in.

ENGLISH GLASS

Crizzled decanter by George Ravenscroft, with decoration "nipt-diamond-waies" and seven vertical pincered and winged ribs. The gilt-metal foot is a later addition. About 1674; $7\frac{7}{8}$in.

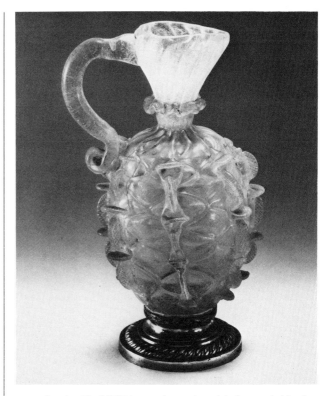

a royal patent in 1575 to produce glass *à la façon de Venise*. Only a small number of drinking glasses (most with diamond-point engraving, and dated) have been attributed to Verzelini on the basis of their form and metal (the earliest dated example, of 1577, is in the Corning Glass Museum, New York) and the decoration is usually considered to be the work of the Frenchman Anthony de Lysle. After about 1592, when Verzelini retired, glass-making *à la façon de Venise* continued under the supervision of Sir Jerome Bowes who, unlike Verzelini, was free to import Venetian examples to satisfy the demands of the wealthy classes.

During the first half of the 17th century, numerous glass-making licences were granted and from 1615 onwards, wood was prohibited as fuel for the furnaces and replaced by coal. A patent was granted to Sir Robert Mansell (1573–1656) at about this time and, based at Verzelini's former Broad Street factory, he soon gained almost total control of the glass industry throughout England, setting up new works and aided by Italian craftsmen (such as Antonio Miotti). He was also the first Englishman to produce mirror glass on a commercial basis.

A SHORT HISTORY

Following the Restoration of Charles II in 1660, Mansell's monopoly was taken over by the Duke of Buckingham, who continued to employ Italian glass-makers in the production of *façon de Venise* and mirror glass at his Vauxhall works, in London. Venetian styles remained popular, as evidenced by the pattern books (now in the British Museum) of John Greene and Michael Measey, whose designs were sent to Murano for execution. However, new glass-making methods were also encouraged at this time, to create a more profitable and independent industry, less reliant on foreign imports. The Glass Sellers' Company was devoted to these aims, and George Ravenscroft (1632–83) was employed for the purposes of research and experimentation. He received a patent in 1674 to create a "perticuler sort of Christaline Glasse" and worked at both the Savoy in London, and at the experimental glass-works at Henley-on-Thames, assisted by the Italian craftsman Da Costa. Ravenscroft's attempts to simulate Venetian *cristallo* may well have been inspired by Antonio Neri's book *L'Arte Vetraria* (see Venetian Glass, p. 57) which had been translated into English by Christopher Merret in 1662. Shortly after this date, Ravenscroft developed a new type of metal called "lead glass" or "flint glass". The latter term was derived from the use of English flints,-which were ground to a powder and added to the glass mixture to increase fusibility. Although flints were soon replaced by sand, the term "flint glass" continued to be employed. At first, Ravenscroft's glass productions were marked by crizzling (See pp. 10 and 47) but this was soon remedied by the important addition of lead oxide which resulted in a stable, durable and brilliant clear glass – considered superior to the fragile soda-lime *cristallo* of Venice – and able to sustain deep, ornamental cutting.

By the late 17th century, the manufacture of lead glass had become widespread. London remained the most important centre and leading exponent of fashionable styles, although other factories were established at Stourbridge, Newcastle, Bristol, Sheffield, Leeds, King's Lynn and elsewhere. The manufacture of plain domestic glass also continued, particularly in the making of dark green and brown bottles for wines and beers (see Bottles, p. 123).

During the 18th century, the German and Bohemian fashion for cut and engraved glass had spread to England, where fine examples were produced about 1740–65. Vessel forms were, on the whole, of a characteristic thickness – solid and weighty – and many new shapes were introduced, exemplified in the frequently changing stems and bowls of drinking glasses, and the novel appearance of items such as glass candlesticks, salt cellars, fruit baskets, custard and jelly glasses etc. (see later chapters). By the mid-18th

Blue-tinted dish gilded with a Greek key pattern along the rim and a stag's head crest (Earls of Verulam) at the centre. Signed on reverse Isaac Jacobs, c. 1800; 7¾in diameter.

century, forms became increasingly light with a greater emphasis on surface ornamentation. This was not only due to the influence of rococo tastes, but also, and more significantly, to the introduction in 1745–6 of new Glass Excise Acts which taxed, by weight, the materials used in glass manufacture.

Bristol (see also p. 214) had become an important glass-making centre by the mid-18th century, and richly coloured vessels were produced here in blue, green, purple, red and opaque white. The term "Bristol blue" is often used incorrectly to describe any blue coloured glass of English origin. The manufacture of blue glass, and of other colours, was widespread throughout England and examples were made at Stourbridge, Newcastle and other northern centres. Isaac and Lazarus Jacobs were well-known manufacturers of glass in Bristol under the patronage of George III, and the decorator Michael Edkins (1734–1811) was also active here during the second half of the 18th century, where he gilded and painted both glass and porcelain wares.

Other important glass decorators of the period were James Giles (1718–80) whose London workshop specialised in gilding white and coloured glass, and the Beilby family (fl. c. 1762–95) who worked at Newcastle and produced distinctive enamelled designs, sometimes with

Royal armorial goblet, enamelled on the bucket bowl with the royal arms and motto of George III, supported on a double-series opaque-twist stem. By William Beilby, who enamelled a series of such glasses, probably to commemorate the birth of the Prince of Wales in 1762. Newcastle, c. 1762; $8\frac{3}{4}$in.

Candlesticks and tea bottles (9in) of opaque white glass, painted with naturalistic floral sprays, butterflies and birds. The bottles have contemporary enamel and gilt-metal tops. Probably south Staffordshire, c. 1755–60.

Nailsea jug of green bottle glass, splashed over the surface with white and red enamels. This early manifestation of the style is usually associated with the Wrockwardine Wood factory in Shropshire, c. 1800–30; 9½in.

gilding, in opaque white and other colours. Coats-of-arms, inscriptions, classical subjects and genre scenes were among the rich and varied range of decorative motifs which they employed. Enamelling was also frequently applied to opaque white glass at centres throughout England, in imitation of porcelain.

The so-called "Nailsea" glass had emerged by the last decade of the 18th century, when John Robert Lucas set up a glass-works at Nailsea, near Bristol. Its manufacture escaped many of the heavy duties placed on finer glass materials which were enforced by the Glass Excise Acts until 1845, and "Nailsea" was a popular and inexpensive form of decorated glass (see also p. 215).

During the first half of the 19th century, fine glass-making was carried out in the Stourbridge and Midlands areas, which became most important by about 1850. However, while many of the London glass-works became less significant during this time, they did not lose their interest for new and fashionable styles completely, as is shown by Apsley Pellatt's introduction of "Crystallo-Ceramie" or "Cameo Incrustations" at his Falcon glass

A SHORT HISTORY

house in Southwark, London, during the 1820s. These "sulphides" were frequently composed of portraits or figures which were made of a white ceramic paste and enclosed in deep cut glass; they were found also on drinking vessels and paperweights.

Eighteenth-century decorative styles remained popular during the early 19th century, and cutting became increasingly pervasive and elaborate. John Ruskin found cut glass "barbarous: for cutting conceals its ductility ..." and this much criticised form of ornamentation soon gave way, albeit temporarily, to simple and relatively sparse facet-cutting from about 1830.

With the repeal of the Glass Excise Act in 1845, glass manufacturers were again able to experiment with various forms and styles of decoration, free from the financial burdens of the last hundred years. The Bohemian industry had, by now, presented English glass-makers with stiff competition, and the products of both Britain and their European rivals were displayed at the Great Exhibition of 1851, held at Crystal Palace in London. This resulted in the rapid assimilation of foreign ideas and styles, as English manufacture widened its scope. New and inventive colours and decorative techniques were developed by firms such as Thomas Webb, and Stevens and Williams, during the second half of the 19th century (see Later Artists and Decorative Styles).

IRISH GLASS

Very little is known about the glass industry in Ireland before the 18th century. Various glass-makers and factories are listed from the late 16th century onwards, but the lack of further documentary evidence and identifiable pieces prevents a detailed historical survey.

Shortly after the introduction of George Ravenscroft's lead glass during the 1670s (see p. 68), a factory was established in Dublin by the Fitz-Simon brothers and Captain Philip Roche and both domestic wares and the "newest fashioned drinking glasses" were manufactured here in the new metal until 1760. Several advertisements appeared during this time for cut glass, and the development in Ireland of this decorative technique was shortly to become of major importance for Irish glass-making.

Throughout most of the 18th century, and earlier, large quantities of glass had been imported into Ireland from England, from places such as London, Newcastle, Bristol and Stourbridge. It was not until 1780 that the situation altered, when the Irish industry benefited from various changes in the law. Coal was no longer taxed when used as fuel for the glass furnaces, export regulations were lifted in that year, and Ireland was now free to trade outside her national boundaries. Perhaps most significant were the Glass Excise Acts of England (see p. 69) which placed heavy financial burdens on manufacturers there. These taxes did not exist in Ireland for many years and, not surprisingly, many English glass-makers set up new factories (some as early as the 1760s) at Belfast, Cork, Dublin and Waterford. The production of lead glass at these important centres is outlined briefly below.

Belfast. About 1771, a factory was established by the Bristol glass-maker Benjamin Edwards, who employed various glass-blowers and decorators from Bristol. Production included a wide range of unadorned and cut domestic wares. The business was taken over by Edwards' son in 1812, and flourished until 1825, when a Glass Excise Act was enforced in Ireland. Although the tax was not as severe as its British counterpart, it nevertheless contributed to a general decline in the Irish industry.

Cork. A factory was recorded in Cork in 1761, but it appears that its years of manufacture were brief. In 1782–3, Hayes, Burnett and Rowe revived the industry, bringing with them workmen from England, and establishing the Cork Glass Company. Its output consisted chiefly of mould-blown domestic wares, particularly decanters, which were occasionally marked with the firm's name (see also Fakes, p. 244). In 1818 the factory closed, but in 1815 the Waterloo Company had been established at Cork by Daniel Foley, and mould-blown decanters (some marked) and jugs were made. Production continued until 1835, when financial difficulties caused by the Glass Excise Act led to bankruptcy.

Dublin. Unlike that of other centres, Dublin's glass industry commenced during the 17th century, with the Fitz-Simon brothers' factory. Others were set up later, such as that of Charles Mulvaney (from 1785 to 1835), and J. D. Ayckbowm, who was active in Dublin from 1802. Dublin glass, however, never achieved the great success of the factories at Cork and Waterford.

Waterford. Glass manufacture began in the early 18th century, but was short-lived. In 1783, William and George Penrose established a factory, and employed John Hill and numerous other glass-makers from Stourbridge. Hill left the firm in 1786 and was replaced by the Englishman Jonathan Gatchell, from which time fine Waterford cut glass was exported widely, to the U.S.A. and elsewhere. After Gatchell's death in 1823, the industry continued to flourish until 1851, when the factory closed (not to re-open for another hundred years). Up until recently, it was claimed that Waterford glass could be identified by a grey or blue tinge in the metal – however, this is now considered an outdated and incorrect theory.

A SHORT HISTORY

Irish glass production reflected English influence during the late 18th and early 19th centuries, in the type of metal, forms and styles of decoration shared by both countries. As a result, it is often difficult to assess whether a piece is of English or Irish manufacture and indeed, with the exception of a few marked pieces, impossible to determine whether from Cork or Dublin, or another Irish factory. Hence, the broad term "Anglo-Irish style" is employed to describe the cut glass wares of the period.

A few novel glass forms evolved in Ireland by the last decade of the 18th century. These include: boat-shaped and circular bowls, probably for holding fruit, many characterised by turn-over rims and supported on stems and feet, showing various forms of cut decoration; the "piggin", a glass imitation of a small wooden pail, with a vertical handle in the form of a tall stave, and used for milk or cream – later adopted by numerous glass factories in England; and butter-coolers or butter-tubs of circular or oval shape, sometimes with two handles and usually accompanied by a cover and stand. Other popular cut glass wares were finger bowls, salt cellars, salad bowls, water jugs, wine glasses, rummers, decanters and chandeliers.

During the 1840s, a new form of cheap imitation cutting, produced by mould-pressing or pressing, was introduced from the U.S.A. (see American Glass). This mass-produced and popular style led to a decline in the demand for fine hand-cut pieces, although by the late 19th century the latter were again preferred. Today, the hand-blown lead glass wares of Ireland – plain, cut or engraved – are famous throughout the world.

Below left Fruit or salad bowl of clear colourless glass, the deeply flanged rim cut decoratively with alternate prisms, and pillar-moulded base. Irish, c. 1780–90.

Below Butter-cooler designed with a cover and matching stand, cut with scallops, diamonds, flutes and splits. About 1800.

Right Clear glass water jug of greyish tone, step-cut across the middle to the top serrated edge, with strawberry diamonds below. Note the thick ridged handle. About 1810.

Below Clear glass piggin, cut with circular "windows" and scallops on the rim and handles. Irish, c. 1820.

A SHORT HISTORY

FRENCH GLASS
The manufacture of clear and stained glass windows for churches and cathedrals was practised continuously in regions such as Lorraine and Normandy from the mediaeval period (see Stained Glass, p. 207). Much flat glass was exported throughout Europe, and the success of this branch of glass-making was repeated in the highly lucrative production of mirror glass by the late 17th century, discussed below. However, in the making of glass vessels, France offered little in the way of new techniques or decorative styles. It was not before the end of the 18th century that the industry was to develop particular skills in the manufacture of fine quality and artistic glass wares, and a further 50 years passed before France achieved an international reputation in this field. This course of events is outlined briefly below. For more detailed discussion of 19th-century craftsmen and styles, see Paperweights, p. 161, and Later Artists and Decorative Styles, pp. 214–35.

Until the 18th century, the manufacture of common glass wares for domestic use followed the traditions of *verre de fougère*, coarse green glass in simple mould-blown shapes (see p. 50). It is recorded that as early as the 14th and 15th centuries, glass-makers from Italy (particularly from Altare) had settled in France and that by the 16th century, glass *à la façon de Venise* was produced extensively throughout the country – at Nevers, Orléans, Paris, in Normandy and in the area of Nantes. Few pieces exist from this period, and it seems that the production of *façon de Venise* in France was not nearly as successful as in other European countries. Although it is not clear why this was so, it does appear that French craftsmen were slow to assimilate the techniques involved in the manufacture of Venetian *cristallo*. As a result, the standard of production of both *façon de Venise* and common glass in France during the 16th and 17th centuries is considered mediocre, and throughout this period the demand for fine glass wares was met by imports from Venice, Germany and the Low Countries.

The most important centres for glass-making *à la façon de Venise* were at Nevers and Orléans. The factory at Nevers was called "a little Murano" by the playwright Thomas Corneille in 1708, and it was here that the fashion for Italian styles prevailed until the 18th century. One curious type of glass that is normally associated with Nevers from the late 16th century onwards took the form of small "toys", consisting of "all sorts of grotesque figures for the decoration of cabinets and chimney pieces", as advertised by the 18th-century glass-maker Jacques Raux. These were produced at the lamp by softening glass rods of different colours and winding them around supportive metal wires, to create a variety of small figurines. The

Small glass figure of the Virgin Mary, worked "at the lamp". Perhaps from Nevers, 18th century.

characters were frequently derived from the Bible and the *commedia dell' arte*. Glass toys were also made at Rouen, Bordeaux, Marseilles, Paris and elsewhere in Europe. It is not surprising, then, that the identification of these pieces is a painstaking, if not impossible, task.

As mentioned previously, the majority of glass wares of the 17th and 18th centuries were of relatively poor quality and the extensive importation of fine pieces had disastrous effects on the glass industry, and on the French economy as a whole. George Ravenscroft's discovery of lead glass in England, during the 1670s, had furthered the decline in glass manufacture both in France and elsewhere in Europe – as imports increased, so the production of glass decreased. One important invention, which was to save the French industry, was the discovery of casting sheets of glass for use in mirrors and windows, developed by Bernard Perrot of Orléans during the last decades of the 17th century (see Looking Glasses, pp. 202–5). The production of mirror glass by this method was so successful that France soon became pre-eminent in this field of manufacture.

During the second half of the 18th century, the manufacture of common glass for domestic use continued to follow the traditions of *verre de fougère*. Although several factories had been established in France for the production of artistic glass wares during the mid-18th century, it appears that their efforts had little effect on the poor state of the industry, and fine pieces continued to be

Pair of clear cut glass vases mounted in ormolu, in the Empire taste. French, c.1810–20; 12¾in.

A SHORT HISTORY

Left French opaline glass in characteristic shades of "milk and water" white, yellow and turquoise. All c. 1840.

Below left Bonbon box cased in yellow glass, with gilt-metal edge and clasp. French, 19th century.

imported from England, Germany and Bohemia. In 1760, the Académie des Sciences offered a prize to anyone who could best analyse the problems which had afflicted the industry for so long. This attempt to rectify the situation and to stimulate production was successful, and was shortly followed by the founding of numerous factories. The most important among these were the Verreries de Sainte-Anne, established at Baccarat in 1765 (known as the Cristalleries de Baccarat by the early 1800s); the Cristalleries de Saint-Louis, also established in Lorraine in 1767; and the Verrerie de la Reine, under the patronage of Marie Antoinette, established at Sèvres in 1784 and transferred to Montcenis

Below Spill vases and goblets, decorated variously with filigree threads, studded florette canes and paperweight bases. By Baccarat, and Saint-Louis, c. 1850; height of goblet 7in.

in 1787. In the late 18th century, these and other factories were chiefly involved in the production of "cristaux blancs, façon et qualité d'Angleterre" – or lead glass in the English style, adorned by elaborate cutting. This mainly derivative period was followed in the early 19th century by the introduction of new decorative styles. The technique of cameo encrustation, for example (later introduced in England by Apsley Pellatt) was developed by Desprez, in Paris, as early as the 1790s, and examples were sold at his shop "À l'Éscalier de Cristal" and made at numerous factories throughout the 19th century. The technique was also to play a significant role in the development of paperweight designs during the 1840s.

By about 1825, the fashion for coloured glass led to the

introduction of opaline (see also pp. 216–18), a semi-opaque glass which was produced initially in a variety of pale pastel shades and later, in brighter colours. Vases, large scent bottles and entire toilette sets were made of opaline glass, and frequently decorated with gilding and other painted motifs, sometimes combined with applied trailing, characteristically in the form of serpents which were entwined around the neck or body of the vessel. Many of the shapes were inspired by contemporary porcelain wares, and were occasionally mounted in ormulu on the handles, feet, bases, lids or stoppers.

Before the mid-19th century, opaline glass, coloured glass in Bohemian styles ("flashed" or "stained"), cut crystal wares and paperweights were all manufactured by the important factories of Baccarat, Choisy-le-Roi (directed by Georges Bontemps and in production 1821–51) and Clichy (established 1837) near Paris, and Saint-Louis. The production of Baccarat and Saint-Louis, in particular, achieved international recognition, and Baccarat continues to make glass of excellent quality.

From the second half of the 19th century onwards, and with the emergence of Art Nouveau, and later Art Deco styles, many new and inventive glass techniques and colour effects were developed by eminent designers, among them Joseph Brocard, who is best remembered for his Islamic-style enamelled wares; Émile Gallé and the Daum brothers, whose cameo glass objects reflect the spirit of Art Nouveau with their soft, muted colours and naturalistic floral designs; Henri Cros, who revived the ancient technique of *pâte de verre*; and, later, René Lalique, whose wide range of mass-produced clear and frosted glass wares and panels – incorporated into architectural schemes – reflect the successful combination of industry and fine craftsmanship (see also Later Artists and Decorative Styles, pp. 214–35).

SPANISH GLASS

Northern Spain

Throughout the 16th and first half of the 17th centuries, the glass of northern Spain was admired internationally, and comparable with the finest products of the Venetian industry.

Catalonia was an important glass-making province with the geographical advantages of being accessible to France, Italy and the East. Barcelona, a great trading city situated on the coast, sustained a guild of glassmakers from the early 1300s. Here and at Palma, on the island of Mallorca, a variety of domestic and decorative glass objects was produced, although few examples survive. At the same time

Enamelled vase in greens and yellows, painted elaborately over the surface with birds and flowers. Barcelona, 16th century; 10¾in.

Bottom Almorrata designed with four sprinkler spouts around the neck, and decorative pincered trails. Catalonia, 17th century.

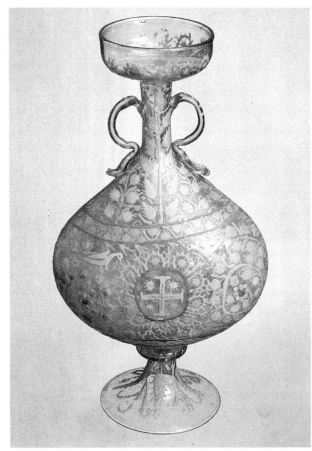

fine wares – such as the highly prized "Damascus glass" with its enamelled motifs – were imported into Catalonia from the Near East.

By the mid-15th century, the glass-blowers of Barcelona had achieved national fame, resulting in the founding of other glass centres (although much remains badly documented) in Mataro and Moncada (north of Barcelona), in the region of Tarragona (south of Barcelona), and along the coast to the province of Valencia, where ordinary wares were made for domestic use. Inland, a factory at Cadalso de Los Vidrios was founded, in the province of Castilla. Throughout the Catalonian region and in Mallorca, uncoloured transparent wares and coloured specimens in blues, purples and yellows were produced. Some examples were made in imitation of semi-precious stones, and enamelled wares were also created, including imitations of

A SHORT HISTORY

Damascus glass with stylised Mudejar designs (half Spanish, half Moorish). New shapes appeared: vases, jars for sweets ("confiters"), salt dishes mounted in silver, and high-stemmed goblets.

From about 1500 to 1650, Catalonian glass was produced extensively *à la façon de Venise*. Numerous Italian glass-makers had settled in regions such as Castilla and Catalonia, teaching their techniques and methods of decoration. By the time Philip II ascended to the throne in 1556, Venetian-style glass was immensely popular and *cristallo* wares, in particular, were widely sought after. The Spanish metal was of an excellent quality due to the presence in it of *barilla* (a species of salt-marsh plant native to Spain, exported to Venice and elsewhere, and an important ingredient in soda-lime glass). Venetian styles to be imitated successfully included ice glass, diamond-point engraving and filigree. The Venetian industry faced stiff competition from Spain and one contemporary commented that "The glass that today is made in Venice is considered excellent, but in many ways that made in Barcelona is better ..."

Some Spanish characteristics were retained with regard to colouring, shape and decoration. Blues, purples and greens were often combined in the same piece or added to uncoloured wares on the covers, handles and feet. The imitation of semi-precious stones also continued and a decoration simulating marble was developed. Gilding existed in two forms, either applied thickly or appearing as specks flecked onto the surface, resembling aventurine glass. Painted subjects were also common, including depictions of angels, figures, animals and birds, sometimes combined with armorial motifs and religious inscriptions. Other patterns show the influence of Mudejar styles, characterised by dotted enamel sections and fish-scale motifs.

After 1650, Spain witnessed political and economic decline, and not surprisingly the glass produced in Catalonia diminished in importance. High standards were no longer maintained and although manufacture continued on a large scale, the domestic wares that were modelled on Venetian prototypes were of poor quality.

A few distinctive national forms evolved, usually attributed to the Catalonian region; they include the *càntaro*, an oddly shaped wine vessel with a large ring handle at the top, two spouts and a decorative bird or flower-shaped finial; the *porrón*, a wine vessel of pear shape with a long spout, and held above the head so that the liquid is expelled in a stream; and the *almorrata*, a rose-water sprinkler characterised by a large neck and four small sprinkler spouts. During the 18th century, the glass output of northern Spain

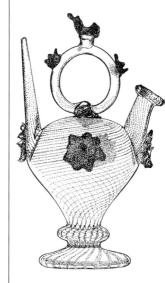

Right Porrón decorated in the filigree style with opaque white threads, and applied trails around the base of the neck. Catalonian, c.1870; 9in.

Below Cántaro in the filigree style, designed with two spouts and large ring handle. Barcelona, 17th century.

included a wide range of drinking vessels, lamps, candlesticks (modelled on silver and brass prototypes), elaborately constructed chandeliers, double cruets for oil and vinegar, vases and trinkets for tourist souvenirs.

Southern Spain

Much of the glass made in southern Spain – in the provinces of Granada, Almería, Murcia and Jaén, in the Andalusian region – does not show the influence of Venice, but rather that of the Moors. Here, a generic style of glass existed up until the 19th century, with wares in shades of green due to impurities present in the metal – a crude, peasant style largely ignored by the rest of Spain and Europe. The majority of examples were intended for everyday use, their basic shapes often decorated elaborately and inspired by Moorish designs taking the form of intricate trailing and threading, loop handles, spiky motifs and applied shells.

However, in the province of Sevilla (also in the Andalusian region) European influences were at work, and apart from *façon de Venise*, Bohemian-style drinking glasses and scent bottles were copied here during the 18th century. Bohemian glass was also imported into Spain during the 1760s, as were pieces from the Netherlands, lead glass from England and mirrors from France.

La Granja de San Ildefonso

To compete with the success of foreign glass manufacturers, Spanish production was actively encouraged. Royal privileges were granted to several glass-makers, and foreign workmen were employed to help establish the industry. Early attempts, however, failed to produce wares of a high quality. In 1728, the royal factory of La Granja de San Ildefonso was founded north-west of Madrid by the Catalonian glass-worker Buenaventura Sit. This glassworks relied almost entirely on royal patronage and after initial financial difficulties it became one of the most successful manufacturers in Spain. By the late 18th century, fine wares were produced here in imitation of English styles, or gilded and wheel-engraved in the Bohemian manner. Other productions included coloured and opaque white glass, often enamelled with simple floral motifs in pastel shades, glass in imitation of semi-precious stones, mirrors and chandeliers.

After 1800, foreign styles were most favoured in Spain. Coloured pieces declined in popularity, while gilded and deeply cut Anglo-Irish pieces remained in vogue. La Granja was sold in 1809 by order of Joseph Bonaparte, newly crowned King of Spain, and without his patronage it was impossible to restore the reputation enjoyed in the 1700s.

Decanter of traditional Anglo-Irish form, made by the Spanish factory La Granja de San Ildefonso. Blown in a fluted mould, and enamelled in bright colours with flowers around the shoulder. About 1775–85; 12½in.

THE LOW COUNTRIES

During the early to mid-16th century, the glass of what is now the Netherlands and Belgium came under the influence of Italian styles, culminating in the extensive manufacture of *façon de Venise*. Later, by the end of the 17th century, when Venetian styles became less popular, the glass of the Low Countries followed the forms and techniques of other nations, notably Germany and England. Throughout this imitative phase of glass-making, however, Dutch craftsmen developed great skills in engraving techniques, which eventually led to the introduction of stipple engraving by the 18th century. Both the assimilation of foreign forms, and the evolution of indigenous decorative styles from the 16th century onwards are traced below.

Façon de Venise

Numerous craftsmen from Murano, and also from Altare on the coast near Genoa, came to the Low Countries during the 16th and early 17th centuries, bringing with them their methods and styles of glass-making. Factories were established throughout the region: in the south (Belgium)

Façon de Venise wine glasses, *left* with an ice glass bowl, *right* decorated with diamond-point engraving on the bowl and foot. The hollow stems are adorned with applied blue glass threads. Netherlands, early 17th century; average height 6½in.

at Antwerp, Liège and Brussels; and in the north (Holland) at Middelburg, Amsterdam, Rotterdam, The Hague, Maastricht, 's Hertogenbosch, and Haarlem. These centres, particularly Antwerp and Liège (notably at the Bonhomme glass-works, which followed Italian styles from about 1680) achieved high standards of workmanship, and in many cases pieces cannot be distinguished from their Italian prototypes. A variety of Italian styles and motifs was employed in the Low Countries including *latticino* and filigree work (often using blue and green coloured threads), aventurine effects, enamelling, gilding – and, generally, the adherence to elaborate shapes and fanciful decoration which involved the manipulation of the glass into innumerable forms. This was reserved especially for the stems of drinking glasses called *Flügelgläser*, with their convoluted "winged" and "serpent" motifs in contrasting colours which were produced continuously throughout the 17th and 18th centuries.

German influence
During the second half of the 17th century, German forms and styles were copied, in addition to those of Venice, including *Römers* (*roemers* in Dutch), *Humpen* and *Passgläser*. Many centres, such as Liège, produced "*verrerie des Allemands*" and both German and Italian glass forms were depicted frequently in Dutch still life paintings of the 17th century.

English influence
During the late 17th century, glass manufacture in the Low Countries moved away from *façon de Venise*, showing a marked preference instead for the lead glass of England, which had been recently discovered by George Ravenscroft. It is recorded that as early as 1680, flint glass *à l'anglaise* was produced at Liège, although it is important to realise that the use of lead as an ingredient in the glass composition was not adopted extensively in the Low Countries, and that the metal was often inferior to its English counterpart. During the early 18th century, factories at Liège, Antwerp and elsewhere produced glass *à la façon d'Angleterre*, notably plainly decorated wine glasses with hollow-knopped, air- or colour-twist stems. Great quantities of English lead glass were also imported into the Netherlands, particularly from Newcastle-on-Tyne, and this dependence on foreign production led rapidly to a decline in the industry. By the 1770s, only one important glass factory remained in Holland, at 's Hertogenbosch, for the manufacture of drinking glasses, while glass-houses at Ghent, Middelburg, Amsterdam and elsewhere were confined chiefly to the production of simple domestic

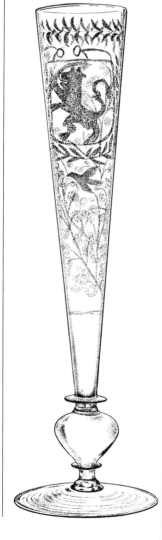

Still-life by the Dutch artist Willem Kalf (1619–93), featuring a glass *roemer* with raspberry prunts, an elaborate *façon de Venise* goblet mounted on a gilt-metal Bacchanalian figure, and a tall flute. Drinking glasses appear commonly in Dutch still-life compositions of the 17th century.

Left Tall flute glass, diamond-point engraved with a lion, bird and foliage.

wares, mirrors and window glass. In the south, English styles continued to be followed at Liège, and in 1743, a new factory was established at Namur for this purpose. But however closely the glass-makers of the Low Countries were able to follow and imitate English prototypes during the 18th century, their glass never achieved the brilliance and durability of its British counterpart, and the absence of lead resulted in pieces which were light in weight, and cloudy or "dirty" in tone. During the 19th century, lead glass in the English style continued to be manufactured in Belgium by the Vonêche glass-works, near Namur (1778–c.1815), and by the Cristalleries du Val-Saint-Lambert founded in 1825 outside Liège which continues today to make finely cut and engraved glass (see Later Artists and Decorative Styles).

Local styles
Several vessel-types developed in the 16th and 17th centuries, including large glass tankards with metal covers, tall elongated "flute glasses" (also popular in Germany), and onion-shaped bottles with long necks, frequently with blue, purple or green coloured handles.

A SHORT HISTORY

In Holland, glass was decorated chiefly by engraving. Imported pieces of English lead glass were particularly well suited to this form of ornamentation and in the hands of Dutch decorators the technique was executed with great skill and ingenuity. Dutch engraving is usually divided into three stylistic categories.

Engraving with a diamond-point was employed during about 1575–1690 by talented amateurs, among them several women. Anna Roemers Visscher (1583–1651) engraved many green glass *roemers* with fruit, flowers and inscriptions, and is best remembered for her free-flowing calligraphic style. Her sister Maria (1594–1649) worked in a similar manner, as did Willem Jacobsz van Heemskerk during the second half of the 17th century. After about 1650, figures, portraits and mythological scenes occur with greater frequency.

Wheel-engraving in the German fashion was employed on many pieces of imported lead glass between about 1690 and 1760. Jacob Sang was the most important decorator to exploit this technique and his depictions of ships and commemorative events occur commonly about 1752–62.

Below left Engraved goblet by the Dutch artist Jacob Sang, inscribed and decorated with a nursery scene to commemorate a birth. About 1740; 6in.

Below Stipple-engraving in the manner of David Wolff (1732–98). The tiny dots of the composition are placed at varying intervals to create effects of light and shade.

One of a pair of Dutch *verre églomisé* pictures in silver and gold with coloured skies, depicting a country house with a balustrade terrace, a horseman, and town landscape in the distance. Signed by Zeuner and dated 1777.

Stipple-engraving with a diamond-point, initially used to a very limited extent by Anna Roemers Visscher during the 1620s, was not employed commonly before the mid-18th century. The practise of stippling in small dots was borrowed from printing techniques and its application on clear glass was developed and mastered by Frans Greenwood (1680–1761) who worked in Dordrecht from 1726. As with wheel-engraving, stipple effects were best achieved on pieces of imported lead glass, by using the diamond-point, or by striking the surface gently with a small hammer carrying a steel needle, to form each dot, creating subtle effects of light and shade. Greenwood borrowed many of his subjects from contemporary prints, and also depicted characters from the *commedia dell' arte*. Another important stipple-engraver was David Wolff (1732–98) whose signed work dates from 1784–95, although a great number of anonymous pieces have been attributed to him. The technique was revived during the 19th century by the Dutch chemist D. H. de Castro, an amateur glass decorator and keen collector of "Wolff" glasses, and is practised today with skill and refinement by Laurence Whistler (b. 1912) in England.

Finally, the technique of *verre églomisé* was employed to great effect by the Amsterdam artist Zeuner, during the early 19th century. (This consisted of thin sheets of gold or silver leaf engraved with a fine needle-point, and placed underneath a protective glass surface.) Zeuner's glass pictures frequently incorporated Dutch and English genre scenes, and he exhibited in England in 1778. (See p. 212.)

AMERICAN GLASS

The glass industry in North America did not become fully established until the 1700s, although there was some manufacture on a limited scale in the 17th century. The first glass-house was founded in 1608–9 with the aid of European craftsmen at Jamestown, on the coast of Virginia, but production was brief and unsuccessful. In 1621, glass-making was again attempted here under the supervision of Italian workmen, and recent excavations at Jamestown have suggested that both bottles and windows were manufactured.

This second factory, however, was soon abandoned and while other glass-houses were established during the 17th century – at Salem in Massachusetts, and along the north-east coast – very little is known of them.

The first important and successful factory was founded in 1739 in southern New Jersey, near Philadelphia, by the German manufacturer Caspar Wistar (1696–1752).

Celery vase of clear lead glass, moulded, free-blown and engraved with leaves and flowers. American, c. 1820–35.

Aquamarine two-handled vase, cream jug and mug in the "South Jersey" style, displaying applied tooled "lily-pad" decoration. About 1835–60.

Numerous glass-makers from Europe were employed here, and production consisted chiefly of a range of clear and coloured domestic wares and window glass. Pieces were frequently decorated with trailing in striped patterns, similar to English "Nailsea" styles, or with applied "lily-pad" motifs on the lower sections of bowls and jugs where the molten glass was trailed on and tooled. Wistar was succeeded by his son Richard in 1752, and the firm continued to flourish until 1780. Domestic glass wares of a similar style were made at this time and until the mid-19th century by other factories in New Jersey, such as that at Millville, in the south, and also in New York and elsewhere in New England. The term "South Jersey type glassware" is used today to describe all of these productions.

During the 1760s, a successful glass-factory was established by the German Henry William Stiegel (1729–85) at Manheim in Pennsylvania; it flourished until 1774. English and German glass-makers were employed here for the production of bottles, window glass and a wide range of domestic wares. In an attempt to compete with European (and particularly British) manufacturers, Stiegel's lead glass was decorated in the most popular and up-to-date styles. Pieces were frequently adorned with enamelled floral and figural motifs, or were engraved and cut in the Bohemian manner. Pattern-moulding (see p. 27) in two

Lacy glass compote, the beehive dish mounted on a round knob pressed stem, and decorated overall with scrolls, leaves and stars. American, 19th century.

and three-piece moulds was also employed for many coloured wares to produce fluted and diamond effects. This style of glass-making, following English and Continental fashions, soon spread to other districts such as Ohio. Few pieces, however, can definitely be ascribed to a specific factory (indeed, many are difficult to distinguish from their European prototypes) and as a result "Stiegel-type glassware" broadly describes these late 18th-century styles.

Throughout the 18th and 19th centuries, much glass was imported into North America from Europe. Nevertheless, while many European styles were imitated, simple mould-blown domestic wares – often tinted blue, green or amethyst – continued to be produced for a home market. The New Bremen Glass Manufactory in Maryland was founded by the German J. F. Amelung in 1784 and was active until 1795. Here a series of dedication pieces of an ambitious nature was produced, with emblems, names and dates engraved on them, and they are easily identified as Amelung glass. Vessels in coloured glass with gilding on the engraving were also made, while site excavations have revealed production of bottles, flasks and simple drinking glasses. Other glass-houses, such as that of William Pitkin in Connecticut, specialised in moulded wares including bottles and spirit flasks decorated with commemorative portraits, popular slogans and inscriptions.

By 1830, the demand for fine glass wares had increased to such an extent that 90 glass-houses were in operation, among them the following:

The New England Glass Company, established in 1818 in East Cambridge, Massachusetts, under the direction of Deming Jarves (1790–1869) and managed by Henry Whitney after 1825. A great variety of wares was made, including mould-pressed and "lacy" glass (see below), paper-weights and lead glass modelled on English and Venetian styles. The firm closed in 1888 due to strikes. (See Libbey Glass Company, below.)

The Boston and Sandwich Glass Company, founded by Deming Jarves in 1825 at Sandwich in Massachusetts. Glass was produced in the styles mentioned above, and mould-pressed lacy wares, sometimes called "Sandwich glass", were a speciality. This firm also closed in 1888.

The Bakewell Glasshouse, established in 1808 by Benjamin and Edward Ensell at Pittsburgh, changing its name in 1813 to the Pittsburgh Flint Glass Manufactory. From 1810 until closure in 1882, fine lead glass tablewares were produced with cut or engraved decoration or pressed into a variety of shapes and patterns. A great number of factories were established in Pittsburgh during the

"Blown three mould" tumblers of pale greyish tone, decorated in relief to imitate Anglo-Irish cutting. Examples were produced in America after c. 1820, by blowing into tripartite moulds. About 1825–35.

A SHORT HISTORY

1820s–30s, and this Pennsylvania city became one of the most important centres for American glass-making.

The Mount Washington Glass Company, established by Deming Jarves in 1837 at south Boston, eventually taken over by William L. Libbey during the 1860s. A variety of mould-blown, mould-pressed and cut wares were produced from c. 1850. The firm was taken over in 1894 by the Pairpoint Manufacturing Company.

The Libbey Glass Company, founded in 1878 when the New England Glass Company was purchased by the Libbey family and continued under their name – re-established in 1888 at Toledo, Ohio, after the closure of the original factory. This glass-house was famous for its cut glass during the late 19th and early 20th centuries, and continues to operate today.

In the early 1800s many factories produced cheap mould-blown imitations of hand-cut pieces in the Anglo-Irish style. The important invention of mould-pressing was introduced in 1827 at the New England Glass Company, and afterwards at the Boston and Sandwich Glass Company by Deming Jarves. This method of operating moulds by machine had an enormous impact on glass-making in the U.S.A., and later in Europe, and a wide range of clear and coloured domestic wares could now be mass-produced cheaply and efficiently by firms throughout the East and Mid-West. Mould-pressed glass was modelled initially on Anglo-Irish cut styles, but soon displayed the elaborate lacy patterns so-called for their intricate and pervasive lace-like motifs and stippled backgrounds, which appeared commonly on household glass during the 1840s and 1850s. Pressed glass was also a medium for political propaganda, with mottoes, emblems and pictures furthering a variety of causes.

During the second half of the 19th century, pressed glass continued to be produced, although the more expensive free-blown, engraved and cut glass tableware was also manufactured for the wealthy. Elaborate "brilliant" cut glass was in great demand c. 1880–1915; this was created by the major glass-factories such as the Libbey Company, and also by small independent companies who specialised exclusively in its elaborate decoration, obtaining the glass blanks (the plain, unadorned shapes) from the larger manufacturers. During this period, several glass-houses such as the Mount Washington Glass Company, were also involved in the production of art glass and many colourful and inventive styles were developed such as Satin, Peachblow, Burmese and Amberina. Louis Comfort Tiffany's iridescent Art Nouveau vessels, stained glass windows and lamps were created for luxury markets from the 1890s onwards (see Later Artists and Decorative Styles).

Favrile glass and bronze "Spider Web" lamp by Tiffany, with a mosaic floral base and oil font. Impressed "TIFFANY STUDIOS NEW YORK" on the base, early 20th century; 27½in.

94

DRINKING VESSELS

The following section includes some of the vessels which have evolved for the consumption of specific drinks. It should be emphasised, however, that the development of specialised glasses is a relatively recent occurrence, and one which took place to a much greater extent in some areas, Venice for example, and England, than in many others. Furthermore, it is not always possible to assign a glass to a particular drink when there is no conclusive evidence that it served only one purpose. Where possible, specific glasses have been dealt with in an international context, but in some cases it has only been appropriate to describe an object with reference to the country of origin.

Throughout these pages it should be borne in mind that in the 18th century, particularly, English drinking vessel forms were widely adapted and imitated, as well as English glassmakers' produce being exported. In the 19th century, however, other countries such as Bohemia took the lead in styles of decoration and colour.

ALE GLASSES
In England, a drinking vessel for ale or strong beer developed c. 1600. Ale was potent and strong in flavour and an appropriately small drinking glass (holding 3–5 ounces) – not unlike one for wine – was designed for its consumption. It was distinctive, however, in the shape of

Left Selection of English ale glasses: *left* engraved with urns and swags in the neo-classical taste, on a facet-cut stem, c. 1775; *centre* engraved with insects, hops and barley, on a double-knopped multi-spiral air-twist stem, c. 1750 (8in); the short ale engraved similarly, on a plain stem, c. 1750.

Right A drinking party, from the illuminated manuscript *Treatise on the Vices*, with written text in Latin. Northern Italy (possibly Genoa), late 14th century or earlier.

DRINKING VESSELS

the bowl which was a slim elongated version of the variously rounded or straight-sided wine bowl. After c.1730, examples are frequently decorated with wheel-engraved, enamelled or gilded "hops and barley" motifs. Designs for bowls, stems and feet follow those for wine glasses – i.e. plain or baluster stems supporting deep bowls (early 18th century); plain, air-twist or opaque-twist stems (c.1750 onwards); and unknopped cut stems supporting ovoid bowls (late 18th century). "Dwarf" ale glasses (holding up to 4 ounces) on short stems were also produced from the early 17th century onwards, and novel giant-sized versions were made over 12 inches high. During the late 18th and 19th centuries, various goblets, tumblers and rummers decorated with a hops and barley motif were also used for ale.

BALUSTERS
Drinking glasses with a baluster stem, inspired by the balustrade of Renaissance architecture (i.e. upright support with a narrow top bulging towards the base). Balusters were produced in England c.1685–1725, usually heavily constructed and made of colourless lead glass with little or no decoration. Baluster stems occur on goblets and wine

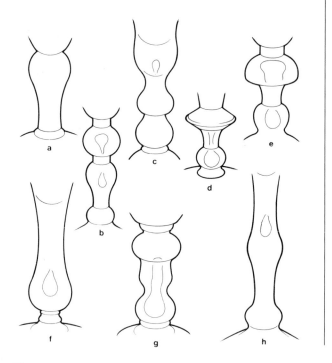

Below left Common types of baluster stems appearing on early 18th-century drinking glasses, showing several knop variations: **a)** plain inverted baluster; **b)** teared ball knop over a teared inverted baluster; **c)** drop knop over a truncated true baluster; **d)** wide angular knop over a teared base knop; **e)** teared true baluster; **f)** plain true baluster enclosing an air bubble; **g)** acorn knop over a short true baluster; **h)** balustroid with swelling waist enclosing a small tear.

Right Selection of early 18th century baluster drinking glasses. *Left to right* Funnel bowl set on a wide angular and basal knop; bell bowl set on a true baluster; round funnel bowl set on a teared mushroom and base knop.

glasses, and less frequently on glasses for ale, gin and cordial. Bowls vary in shape but are almost always thickly constructed at the base, sometimes with a "tear". Feet were thickly folded after c.1690, or sometimes domed and folded.

At least nine distinct categories of baluster stem exist, the majority having one or more knops of different shapes and sizes. The inverted baluster (bulging at the top) was the first stem to appear c.1685 (and also adopted in Germany c.1720–30), either plain or knopped, followed by numerous others including the drop knop c.1690–1710, the angular knop c.1695–1715 and the true baluster c.1710–30 which can be seen on the well-known "Kit-Cat" glasses in the painting by Sir Godfrey Kneller (National Portrait Gallery, London).

A lighter, elongated version of the baluster stem is the balustroid, occurring on English drinking glasses c.1725–60. Examples were sometimes enamelled, or engraved by Dutch artists on the bowl.

DRINKING VESSELS

BEAKERS

A type of drinking vessel, usually characterised by a flat base and cylindrical body, often widening at the top. Occasionally it is mounted on a stemmed foot or on bun feet and after c. 1500 beakers sometimes had a lid or cover.

Fragments of beakers dating from as early as the 15th century BC have been found in Iraq and it is thought that similar vessels were used around the same time in ancient Egypt. By the 1st century AD, concave-shaped beakers (the sides inward-curving from top to bottom) were made throughout the Roman empire, the majority of unrefined green glass. Mould-blown beakers characterised by high relief bosses have been found as far apart as Syria, Pompeii and southern France.

By the 5th century, two distinctive types of beaker were made throughout Europe. The first was the cone beaker, an elegantly styled drinking glass with a narrow, cone-shaped body tapering to a very small but impractical base. When empty of liquid the cone could be inverted for standing. Examples found in England were of common green glass, with bold trailed decoration; a taller version, called a

Daumenglas or *Daumenhumpen* "thumb glass" of barrel-shape, designed with circular indentations for inserting the fingers, and bands of notched trails at the top and bottom. Of greenish coloured *Waldglas*, German or Dutch, late 17th century.

Milchglas beaker with moulded octagonal sides, enamelled with stylised leaves. Central European, c. 1750.

Berkemeyer of blue-tinted glass, decorated with prunts and an applied frilled foot-ring. Probably Rhineland, c. 1560–80.

DRINKING VESSELS

Spitzbecher, was made in Rhineland regions from the 5th to the 7th centuries. The claw beaker is so-called for its peculiar decoration of numerous claw shapes which protrude from the sides of the vessel. Many have been excavated in Britain from Anglo-Saxon graves and in Seine and Rhine areas, where they are known as *Rüsselbecher* (the claws resemble elephants' trunks). Claw beakers continued to be produced during the early mediaeval period in Europe.

The manufacture of beakers was most concentrated in northern European areas from the 5th century onwards. Numerous types evolved, of which the following were typical: the shellfish beaker (or *Konchilienbecher*), an early type made in the Cologne area and aptly named for its shellfish decoration placed in circular bands around the body; the bell beaker, so-called for its shape, and made in the 5th–8th centuries; the dolphin beaker, decorated with blobs in the form of fish tails and fins; the *Humpen*, of large cylindrical form, decorated with blobs and trailed zig-zag motifs (from the 16th century onwards, *Humpen* were made in large numbers, usually enamelled with figural scenes and armorial motifs); the *Nuppenbecher* (literally "drop beaker"), decorated with applied drops of glass and produced from the 14th century onwards; the *Maigelein*, frequently decorated with mould-blown patterns and popular from the middle ages onwards; the *Stangenglas* ("pole glass"), a tall beaker mounted on a wide foot; a similar version, the *Passglas*, divided into sections by trailed threads on the surface of the vessel, was intended for communal drinking.

During the mediaeval period, the majority of beakers were made of common green glass in the *Waldglas* tradition (see p. 50) but by the late 16th and the 17th centuries, examples became more elaborate – boldly enamelled on clear colourless glass, or deeply coloured with gilded and cut surfaces, sometimes mounted in silver. Many beakers were made in Germany, Bohemia and Austria during the 19th century, and they continued to be richly adorned.

Beakers in characteristic Venetian styles were also made in Venice and exported from the late 15th century; in such places as England and Germany they were in great demand.

In England, beakers were produced from the late 16th century when numerous examples were modelled on silver prototypes, with large foot-rings. Designs for beakers were sent by the London Glass Sellers' Company (c. 1667–73) to Venice, where they were made for the English market. Both glass and silver models, however, declined in popularity during the early 18th century.

BRANDY GLASSES
Brandy, made in France from distilled wine or grapes, was

Pair of clear glass balloon-shaped brandy glasses. Early 20th century; 5½in.

popular among the wealthy in 18th-century England. It is likely that ordinary small tumblers of cylindrical form were used from the late 17th century onwards. Such glasses were featured in the design books of John Greene c. 1670 and brandy glasses were also mentioned in George Ravenscroft's price list of 1677, where they were described as "ribbed and plain". Surprisingly, there is no reference to brandy tumblers in 18th-century advertisements, but it is probable that an assortment of small tumblers and rummers continued to be used, with no specific type as yet developed.

The typical brandy glass of today – a large balloon-shaped bowl on a stemmed foot – made its first appearance at the turn of this century. The bowl is held to warm the brandy as it is swirled around to let the vapours rise; some recent examples can be fixed to a metal rack and placed over a flame for gentle heating.

DRINKING VESSELS

CHAMPAGNE GLASSES

Champagne was exported from France to England in the late 17th and the 18th centuries, but champagne glasses were only seldom referred to in 18th-century advertisements, where they were described simply as "flutes" (i.e. tall and narrow, and equally well suited to fine ales and cider) or "egg champagnes" (probably of goblet form with an ovoid bowl). It is likely that both types were of fine quality glass (possibly with vines engraved or enamelled on the bowl), in keeping with the exclusive nature of the drink.

The *tazza*-shaped champagne glass popular today, with a wide shallow bowl, was referred to by Disraeli in 1832 as "a saucer . . . mounted upon a pedestal of cut glass". This type (holding 4–6 ounces) probably developed c. 1830 and has been manufactured up to the present time, although flutes remain the more appropriate alternative as they do not allow the bubbles in the drink to escape so readily.

COIN GLASSES

Drinking glasses which enclose a coin (or coins) in the hollow part of the stem, or in the foot, are thought to have originated in Venice by the mid-17th century. Such novelties were probably intended as souvenirs, with portraits of contemporary Doges on the faces of the coins. In England, stemmed coin glasses do not appear before c. 1680 during the reign of Charles II, and examples were produced thereafter mainly for commemorative purposes. Coin tankards and jugs of glass were popular during Victorian times, to mark events such as the Great Exhibition of 1851 or the Jubilee of 1887.

It is important to realise, however, that the date of the coin may precede that of the vessel.

Right Flute glass with drawn trumpet bowl, set on a multi-spiral air-twist stem and conical foot, for wine or champagne. English, c. 1750; 7½in.

Left, centre Coin goblet (flanked by contemporary drinking glasses). The large round funnel bowl set above two collars and a hollow blown merese decorated with raspberry prunts, containing a groat of 1678. The high conical foot is folded. English, c. 1700; 7in.

DRINKING VESSELS

English cordial glasses. *Left to right* Funnel bowl set on a double-series opaque-twist stem, c.1770; trumpet bowl set on a double-series opaque-twist stem having a central gauze core, c. 1770; green-tinted glass set on a diamond faceted stem, c.1785; ovoid bowl set on a double-series opaque-twist stem, c.1770.

CORDIAL GLASSES

Cordials were potent alcoholic drinks made from various fruits, herbs and spices, popular in England since the early 1600s. They were consumed from small ordinary drinking glasses (reserved also for gin and rum) or "drams" – a term which continued to be employed for cordial glasses during the 18th century. By 1730–40, the serving of cordials after tea became fashionable in wealthy homes, and cordial glasses were designed to complement fine porcelain tea services. These have small bowls (holding $1–1\frac{1}{2}$ ounces) and are mounted on tall thick stems. Eighteenth-century examples follow the decorative styles of contemporary wine glasses, with variously shaped bowls and stems (initially knopped, then plain, air-twist, opaque-twist and cut) on domed or folded feet. In addition, a cordial glass for ratafia (and probably other sweet cordials) developed c.1740–80; this consisted of a small slender flute mounted on a tall thick stem and plain foot, and is also known as a flute cordial. Like many cordial glasses, the flute was often decorated with delicate engraving. By c.1880, cordial glasses were

Historical cup plate of lacy glass, decorated with the American Eagle and Star design. Midwestern, c. 1830.

almost entirely superseded by small rummers.

In Bohemia, small opaque-white glasses for cordials and liqueurs were manufactured during the 18th century.

CUPS

A small bowl-shaped drinking vessel, with or without handles, usually with a foot-ring or mounted on a stemmed foot. A number of cups for specific beverages had evolved by the early 18th century (see below), although various domestic and luxury glass specimens have survived of Roman manufacture, notably the well known cage cups with their pierced network surrounds, and the mould-blown "Circus" and "Victory" cups decorated with pictorial scenes (described on p. 38). Domestic cups and beakers, or *Maigelein*, were made of *Waldglas* in Rhineland regions up to the 15th century, and in the same century large (5–6 in high) standing cups and goblets, sometimes called "wedding cups", were manufactured in Venice to commemorate marriages. Later, cups with matching saucers were produced for luxury markets, the majority of porcelain but some of glass.

Tea-bowl. Small handleless cup for drinking tea, designed with a saucer and manufactured in China from the 18th century onwards, frequently of opaque white glass with enamelled decoration to simulate contemporary porcelain. Chinese-style tea bowls were also imitated in Europe from c. 1740 – particularly in Germany and Bohemia for export markets – many of opaque white glass with brightly speckled or combed decoration, or sometimes painted with classical scenes in the manner of Meissen porcelain. During the Biedermeier period c. 1820–40, tea-bowls of Lithyalin and Hyalith glass were produced at Potsdam, occasionally

Lithyalin cup and saucer of marbled glass, gilded with *chinoiserie* designs. Bohemian, c. 1830.

Pair of Chinese wine cups and saucers of "boudoir pink" colour, c. 1850.

gilded with *chinoiserie* designs. In England, relatively few glass tea cups were made, but some of clear cut glass were advertised from c. 1730; some later examples, following filigree styles with applied coloured bands around the rims of bowls, were produced in the Bristol area c. 1790, and contemporaneously in Venice. A few handled cups were also made by Apsley Pellatt c. 1820, decorated with cameo incrustations.

Trembleuse. French term for a cup and saucer (the latter designed with a deep central depression or well for securing the cup), used for drinking tea, coffee, chocolate and bouillon. Examples were made in Venice c. 1720–1800,

coloured opaque white with painted pictorial scenes, or of aventurine and chalcedony glass.

Wine cup. Small handleless cup – smaller than a tea-bowl – for drinking wine, manufactured in China from c. 1736 onwards, of brightly coloured opaque glass.

Cup plate. Small glass dish produced exclusively in the U.S.A. during the 19th century, used for resting a dripping tea cup after the hot liquid had been poured from the cup to its saucer from which the cooled beverage was then drunk. Large numbers were made of pressed glass after c. 1830, and over 1,000 different decorative designs have been identified.

GOBLETS

Large stemmed glasses, about 10 in high or taller, the bowl variously shaped and with or without a cover. Most examples were highly ornate, catering to luxury markets as presentation gifts or commemorative wares (and less for drinking purposes). Early goblets are rare: a few colourless examples with wheel-cut decoration have survived of 9th century Persian manufacture and later some outstanding enamelled goblets were made by Islamic craftsmen during the 13th and 14th centuries (some were brought by Crusaders to Europe, where they were highly prized). It was not until the 15th century, however, that goblets appeared more commonly, first in Venice and thereafter throughout Europe under the influence of *façon de Venise*. Early Venetian examples were of rich coloured glass, enamelled and gilded with biblical subjects or contemporary processional scenes and portraits, often designed to commemorate marriages. Later, when the *cristallo* glass came to be favoured in the early 1500s, enamelling became restrained and the metal itself was elaborately manipulated on the stems of goblets, with coloured loops and pincered threads, into extravagant and fantastic forms resembling winged beasts, or as large floral medallions. Other goblets were adorned with filigree threads (a style which persisted into the 19th century) mounted on stems with bulbous knops of spherical shape or in the form of lions' masks. Standard Venetian types were imitated elsewhere from the 1500s onwards, in keeping with the popularity of *façon de Venise* – particularly in the Low Countries, Spain, and in Germany where goblets were sometimes enamelled with armorial motifs.

In England, the commemorative goblets (c. 1577–86) attributed to the London-based Giacomo Verzelini demonstrate Venetian influence with their bulbous moulded stems. By the late 17th and early 18th centuries, however, goblets of the new lead glass reflect the gradual transition away from Venetian delicacy and fantasy in favour of plainer surfaces and sturdier construction. English goblets were of basic design, although after c.1750 surface decoration could be elaborate – as in the enamelled armorial goblets of the Beilbys, c.1762–75, or those with engraved commemorative scenes (frequently decorated by Dutch craftsmen). In Ireland, goblets were made at Waterford and other notable factories c.1780–1825, engraved or deeply cut in characteristic style.

Elsewhere in Europe, goblets were a pervasive form from the 1500s onwards, and following the period of *façon de Venise* a variety of national types and decorative styles developed. In Germany, a covered goblet (10–24in high) known as a *Pokal* was manufactured c.1680–1850; it was

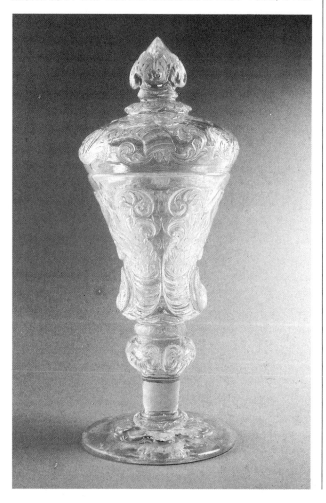

Hochschnitt goblet and cover, the flared bowl in the form of a cornucopia, wheel-engraved in relief with acanthus sprays and birds. From the workshop of Friedrich Winter (d.1712), late 17th century; 11in.

intended for toasting at celebrations and was engraved on the bowl according to period styles. Novelty bell goblets – the bowl mounted on a bell-shape, replacing the stemmed foot – were produced in the Netherlands and Germany from c.1650 onwards, as were the rarer "acorn" goblets with large hemispherical bowls and dome-shaped covers. In Bohemia, two-tiered and ordinary covered goblets were a favourite form produced over a long period of time and engraved by master craftsmen; they were commonly flashed and engraved during the 19th century. In Holland, examples were stipple- and wheel-engraved with elaborate pictorial scenes, frequently executed on lead glass goblets imported from England during the 18th century.

Below right Bohemian two-tiered goblet, late 17th century.

Below left Acorn goblet with coiled surface design, set on a lion's mask stem. Netherlands, 16th–17th century.

DRINKING VESSELS

Left Façon de Venise blue-tinted goblet, decorated over the surface with diamond-point engraving in the form of scrolling flowers, and moulded and gilded lions' masks. Probably Barcelona, c. 1580.

Below Armorial tankard, enamelled in bright colours with an angel and elaborate coat-of-arms, and dated 1614. Bohemia or Franconia; 7⅓in.

Right Tankard of Milchglas enamelled in Schwarzlot style with stags in a wooded landscape, and mounted in silver-gilt. Probably Franconia, dated 1685; 7in.

Below right English beer mugs, left of tapering cylindrical form inscribed and engraved with hops and barley, right bell-shaped with gadrooned lower section and reeded scroll handle (5in). Both second half of the 18th century.

In the U.S.A., *Pokals* were introduced by the German glass-maker John Frederick Amelung, and manufactured at his New Bremen Glass Manufactory c. 1790. Thereafter, goblets of various styles and decoration were produced widely, in imitation of European styles or pressed and patterned with thumbprint and other characteristic designs.

MUGS AND TANKARDS

For beer, cider and other long drinks, made in many parts of Europe since the 16th century (and by the late 18th century in North America). The terms have often been interchanged to describe a stemless vessel resting on a flat base, with a handle on one side, and a circular rim. Examples were frequently designed with a detachable cover or hinged lid, made of glass or metal, and these, together with those with a capacity of about one quart are more appropriately labelled tankards. Many display elaborate decoration,

suggesting that their manufacture was intended for commemorative purposes, or as souvenirs.

Mugs and tankards were produced in greatest numbers in Germany, Bohemia and central Europe from the late 16th century onwards. They were made of colourless and coloured glass, often gilded and enamelled with detailed pictorial designs (biblical scenes, portraits, hunting subjects, etc.) and armorial emblems. By the 19th century, Bohemian mugs were frequently cased in two or more colours, and were mass produced for export.

In England, glass tankards were seldom produced but mugs were made c. 1680 onwards. Most were of metal and stoneware, however, although glass rummers were also used commonly in taverns. During the 18th century, a few glass mugs were engraved with apples or hops and barley motifs, but it was not until the introduction of pressed glass techniques c. 1830–40 that examples were mass-produced for use in public houses.

Mugs made in Spain during the late 1700s, at La Granja de San Ildefonso, were of crystal or opaque white glass, enamelled and/or cut with floral patterns. At this time a few covered tankards were made at Venice, and in North America mugs were made in a variety of colours and styles, in New Jersey and throughout the East Coast area.

DRINKING VESSELS

POSSET POTS AND GLASSES

Made in England from the 17th century, of various shapes and sizes, but generally in the form of a straight-sided or rounded cup with two loop handles, a curved spout and sometimes a cover. They were used for drinking posset – a semi-liquid food consisting of hot milk curdled by wine or ale, with breadcrumbs and spices – and possibly other drinks such as the thicker caudle (alcohol-based, with bread or oatmeal). Posset was consumed from the spout, which avoided contact with the curdled milk on the surface of the drink and was probably of additional value to invalids as a type of feeding-cup. Large posset pots of lead glass (capacity about 15 ounces) were made by Ravenscroft, a few bearing the raven's head seal, c. 1676–78, but during the period 1700–1750 these were much rarer. Some resemble jelly glasses (capacity about 2–3 ounces), perhaps indicating a change in the type or consistency of the drink. It is thought that a few posset pots were made in Venice for the English market, prior to the mid-18th century.

Above Two-handled posset pot of clear lead glass. English, c. 1710; 4½in.

Left Römer of green-tinted glass with characteristic coiled foot and raspberry prunt decoration on the hollow stem. Netherlands, 17th century; 5¾in.

Rummer, engraved on the bowl with hops and barley and the initials C B, mounted on a square "lemon-squeezer" foot. English, c. 1800.

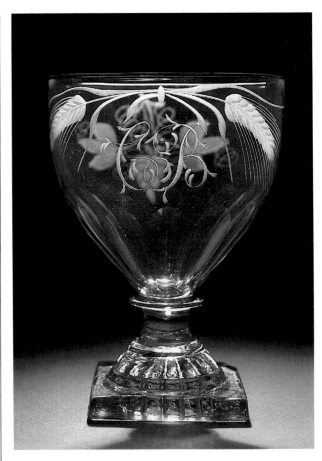

RÖMERS AND RUMMERS

The German *Römer* is a distinctive and widespread form of drinking glass used for Rhenish white wine from the 16th century onwards. The typical design consists of a large spherical bowl mounted on a wide hollow stem decorated with applied blobs. These "prunts" were most frequently impressed with raspberry motifs, but sometimes moulded into lions' masks, or drawn out to a fine point in a way resembling earlier *Waldglas* styles. The hollow foot was usually flared and built up of threads of glass wound around the exterior of a conical wood or metal core (which was subsequently removed), although by the 18th century the foot was blown and encircled by threads. This basic style of *Römer* was popular from the 16th century onwards – made of green coloured *Waldglas* or clear colourless soda glass – throughout Rhineland regions, central Europe, and briefly

DRINKING VESSELS

in England (c. 1678–81 in the new lead glass, and c. 1750 when examples were tinted green in imitation of *Waldglas*). *Römers* were depicted frequently in 17th-century Dutch still-life paintings, and from this period onwards many were designed with large bowls, which were frequently engraved. Examples are manufactured today, and are still reserved for drinking Rhenish wines.

The large-bowled and short-stemmed drinking glass known as a rummer evolved gradually in England, initially inspired c. 1660s–1680s by its German prototype (from the name of which the term rummer probably derived). But by the early 1700s the rummer was distinctive and bore little resemblance to its continental predecessor. Rummers (usual capacity about ½ pint) were used in English taverns throughout the 18th and 19th centuries for numerous long drinks such as mulled wines, beer, sack or cider, with smaller versions for gin and other spirits (and also, later, for rum – the drink has no connection with the term rummer). Examples are of various designs, but usually with a large dominating bowl that appears somewhat disproportionate in relation to its short stem and small foot. Bowls were commonly ovoid in shape before c. 1790, but thereafter other styles were adopted according to period tastes, and decorated with fluting and/or wheel-engraved pictorial scenes and portraits. Stems were short and from the late 18th century styles followed those for wine glasses. Feet were plain and circular, or heavy and square by the last quarter of the 18th century. All of these styles and variations persisted until the late 19th century.

TOASTING GLASSES
Delicate drinking glasses (capacity 2–4 ounces), made of soda or lead glass and popular in Europe for toasting c. 1725–50. Early examples were designed as slender flutes, afterwards with trumpet-shaped bowls tapering into very thin and tall stems (less than ⅛ inch thick) for breaking between the fingers after the toast to prevent the glass from being used again. The majority are undecorated, although some were engraved on the bowl, with slender opaque-twist stems. By c. 1750, the custom of toasting became less exclusive and special glasses were no longer produced.

TOAST-MASTER'S GLASS
A deceptive drinking glass produced in England c. 1750 onwards, used by toast-masters to remain sober whilst officiating at social gatherings. Examples resemble cordial glasses, with tall thick stems, but the inside of the thick-walled bowl is V-shaped to reduce its capacity (under ¾ ounce).

Above Toasting glass of soda metal, with drawn trumpet bowl and plain stem. Antwerp; c.1700; 7½in.

Above right Deceptive toast-master's glass, the thickened ogee bowl having an interior V-shaped depression, mounted on a double-series opaque-twist stem and conical foot. English, c.1760; 5½in.

Right Firing glass of solid construction, the ogee bowl set on a double-series opaque-twist stem and thick terraced foot.

Far right Pair of "Lynn" clear glass cylindrical tumblers with stepped sides, and low kicks at the base. The stands have narrow and broad corrugations, in characteristic style. King's Lynn or Norwich, c.1765.

DRINKING VESSELS

FIRING GLASSES
Short, sturdy drinking glasses on thick stems and solid feet (about 4 in high), produced in England from c. 1740 and used for drinking and rapping loudly on tables to silence the drinkers in anticipation of a toast or song. The term "firing" glass was coined as the thumping sounds resembled gunshots. The glasses, solidly constructed of necessity, had feet up to $\frac{1}{2}$ inch deep, and thickly walled bowls of various shapes. They are unadorned or sometimes engraved with masonic emblems or Jacobite slogans and motifs. The one illustrated has a double-series opaque-twist stem.

TUMBLERS
A drinking vessel without a stem, handle or foot, resting on a flat base, resembling a handleless mug. Tumblers of various shapes and sizes (with giant versions 10 inches high) were produced commonly throughout Europe from the early 1700s onwards. Decorative tumblers were made in Spain c. 1775, enamelled or cut; in Germany, Bohemia and Austria, of *Zwischengoldglas* c. 1730–55 (the best early in this period), or with pictorial scenes in translucent enamels by Samuel Mohn and son in the early 1800s; and in England, engraved with Jacobite slogans c. 1740 and later with hops and barley motifs and/or commemorative scenes from c. 1800 onwards. Many were also cut in Anglo-Irish styles c. 1780–1820, and later mould-pressed in imitation of hand-cutting.

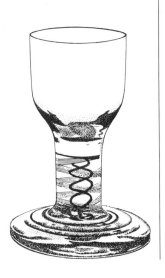

DRINKING VESSELS

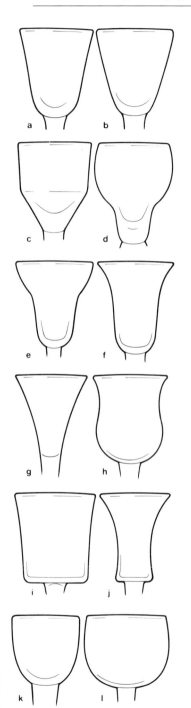

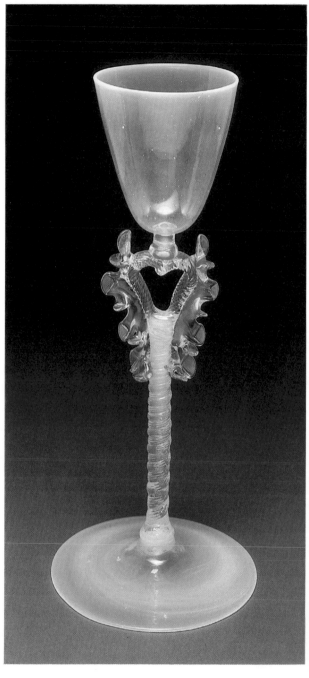

WINE GLASSES

Manufactured widely in an unlimited range of shapes, sizes and styles, and frequently made in sets. Though by no means restricted to Venice and England, the major developments in the forms and styles of the wine glass occurred in these two places, and were copied and interpreted in other manufacturing countries.

Far left Common bowl shapes found on drinking glasses: a) small round funnel; b) flared; c) ogee; d) double-ogee; e) pan-topped; f) bell; g) drawn trumpet; h) thistle; i) bucket; j) waisted bucket; k) small ovoid; l) cup

Left Venetian "opal" wine glass, 17th century.

Above Façon de Venise "winged" wine glass, probably northern Europe, 17th century.

Above right Venetian and *façon de Venise* wine glasses. *Left* on moulded lion's mask stem; *centre* on hollow knopped stem possibly from Liège; and *right* resting on collar and baluster stem. All 17th century.

Venice

During the 16th and 17th centuries, Venetian *cristallo* glass was in great demand throughout Europe and wine glasses were among the many wares to be exported and copied. Shapes of bowls, stems and feet vary, but the majority of examples demonstrate an overall delicacy and fluidity of form in keeping with the inherent ductile qualities of soda glass. Free-standing threads of clear and coloured glass were looped and scrolled elaborately around the bases of bowls and stems. These popular decorative motifs, often resembling wings, or shaped fancifully into dragons, serpents and grotesque figures, are also found on contemporary *tazze* and other vessels. Alternatively, stems were moulded and gilded with lions' masks, or bunches of grapes, on the hollow bulbous protrusions or knops. Early Venetian wine glasses are often clear and colourless, although filigree styles were employed occasionally on bowls, stems and feet, consisting of opaque-white threads twisted within the metal to create complicated lace-like patterns. In the late 17th and the 18th centuries, styles became increasingly elaborate. Bowls of richly coloured glass (frequently blue, amethyst and emerald green), diamond-engraved with flowers, were mounted on clear

DRINKING VESSELS

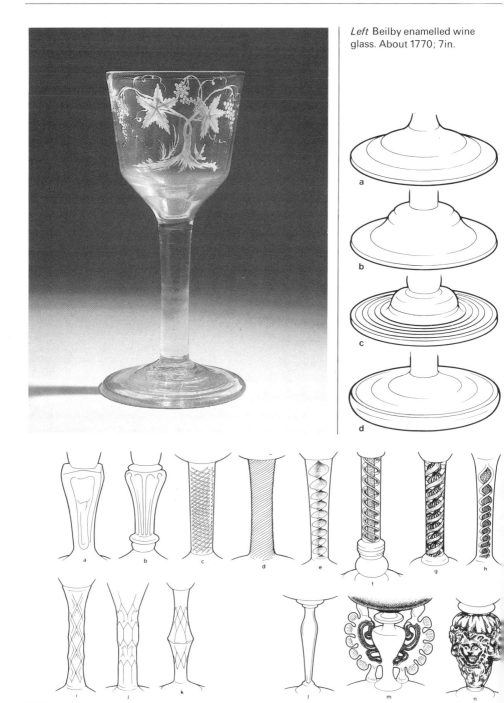

Left Beilby enamelled wine glass. About 1770; 7in.

Right Two air-twist stem wine glasses displaying multi spirals (one incorporating knops) and *right* a "gauze corkscrew". English, c. 1750.

Left The main types of foot, found on drinking glasses and other objects included the: **a)** folded conical; **b)** domed; **c)** domed and terraced; and **d)** thick circular, as found on firing glasses.

Left, below After balusters (see p. 98), other 18th-century stem types developed in England (thereafter adopted widely) including the *moulded pedestal or Silesian,* showing variations **a)** 4-sided, c. 1715 and **b)** 8-sided, c. 1745; **c)** *air-twist,* showing a multi-spiral pattern, c. 1750; **d)** *incised-twist,* c. 1750; *opaque- and colour-twist,* showing variations **e)** single corkscrew, c. 1760, **f)** double-series twist, c. 1760, **g)** another double-series twist, c. 1760, and **h)** reticulated twist corkscrew, c. 1770; *facet-cut,* showing variations **i)** diamond faceted, c. 1780, **j)** hexagonal faceted, c. 1785, and **k)** faceted with swelling waist knop, c. 1785.
   Fashionable Venetian and *façon de Venise* stem types of the 16th and 17th century included the **l)** plain hollow baluster; **m)** hollow baluster flanked by scroll-shaped handles and pincered denticulations; and **n)** the moulded lion's mask.

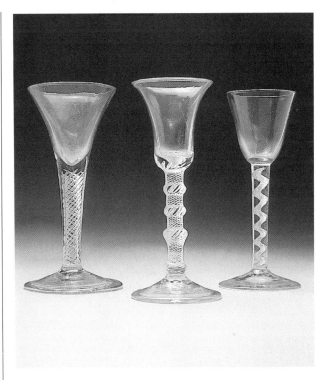

stems decorated with free-standing threads of contrasting shades (alternatively, clear bowls appeared on coloured stems). Coloured glass flowers and leaves are also popular motifs, applied prominently to the surfaces of stems.

England

Large numbers of Venetian glasses were exported to England, and imitated there, until Ravenscroft's discovery of lead glass. From c. 1680 onwards, English manufacturers moved away from ornate Venetian styles in favour of simpler and sturdier forms, such as the baluster glasses distinctive for their thick and bulbous stems. The 18th century gave rise to many new and inventive styles, illustrated by frequent changes and modifications in the shapes (and combinations) of bowls, stems and feet, and by the fashionable and decorative treatments of the stems. Many of the changes were influenced directly by the Glass Excise Acts of 1745 and 1777 (see p. 69). As a result, wine glasses and other wares became lighter and smaller – no longer designed with the heavy and thick stems and feet of earlier years, but now demonstrating the greater use of surface decoration (enamelling, gilding and engraving), and

DRINKING VESSELS, SERVING DRINKS

featuring twist and faceted stems. Among the most distinctive wine glasses were those with opaque-coloured twist stems incorporating threads of white, red, blue, green, brown, purple or yellow, combined and twisted into an infinite variety of patterns and complementing effectively the brilliance and clarity of the surrounding lead glass. Plain but richly coloured wine glasses were also produced from c. 1760 in the popular "Bristol" styles. After the repeal of the Excise Acts in 1845, a wider range of wine glasses was manufactured, reflecting Victorian tastes for new colours and surface effects. See line drawings for the chronological development of characteristic shapes and styles. (See also the entries for other drinking vessels.)

BOTTLES

Glass bottles have been manufactured since earliest times. The ancient Egyptians produced small core-formed bottles for essences and oils, and following the introduction of glass-blowing, the Romans created an extensive range of multi-purpose free- and mould-blown bottles used for the storage and transportation of liquids, or to contain the ashes of the deceased. During the Islamic period, pattern-moulded sprinkler bottles were manufactured widely for the slow pouring of perfumed essences, and in the forest glass-houses of mediaeval Europe such as those of the Weald and Seine–Rhine regions, thinly blown bottles of common green glass were produced with "kick" bases for greater stability. From the 16th century onwards, decorative glass bottles were made in Venice for a luxury market but it was not until the early 17th century that the commercial production of specific types evolved internationally.

Left, above Opaque-twist stem wine glasses, popular in England from c. 1760; average height 6in.

Left Colour-twist stem wine glasses, all English c. 1760, showing some of the range of colours including white, blue, yellow, green and turquoise. On the *left* the bowl is decorated by Beilby. The stem on the *right* is a mixed air and turquoise twist.

Above Swiss bottle enamelled with the arms of Swiss cantons. Inscribed and dated 1793, 11⅔in.

Right Medicine bottles and phials of clear and green-tinted glass, all excavated in the City of London on the sites of chemists' shops. About 1620–1720; smallest bottle 1½in.

SERVING DRINKS

Bottles for wine

In England a very solid bottle, made of blackish-green glass, was first produced soon after 1650. It was strong enough to be used for transporting wine, without the wanding which had until now given some protection to glass bottles, while the colour protected the contents from light. Its advantages were soon recognised abroad, and by the early 18th century it was the standard type in most European countries as well as in America. It replaced the earthenware and stoneware jugs which were used to carry wine from the cask to the table, and many early glass bottles reflect the influence of pottery designs; some had a handle and an initialled and/or dated seal – these are known as serving or decanter bottles. Glass seals (applied circular glass pads, impressed with a metal stamp) were used commonly on bottles from the mid-17th century onwards, the seal indicating the name of the tavern or the initials of the wine merchant or drinker. These bottles were frequently dated, the earliest surviving sealed bottle dating from 1657. Personal sealing remained popular in England until c. 1835, when mechanised processes were adopted for impressing the name and manufacturer of the drink upon the vessel. Sealed bottles were also produced throughout Europe and America by the early 18th century – for mineral waters, spirits, liqueurs and wines.

The shapes of wine bottles changed considerably over the 150 years following their introduction. The first type,

Right Common wine bottle shapes, from the late 17th to mid-18th century. *Below* Shaft and globe. *Top, left to right* Onion shape; shouldered; cylindrical.

Below Late 18th-century magnum bottles, each having an applied seal stamped with a name, date or family crest. English, smallest bottle 9in.

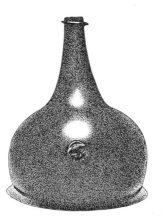

known as the shaft and globe, persisted until at least c.1700, by which time the tall neck had been shortened and the spherical body become more dome-shaped. Such bottles could not be stacked, but were laid out in sand or sawdust on the floor of the cellar. From c.1715–25 the squat rotund shapes of previous years gradually disappeared and bottles became increasingly elongated and straight-sided, finally cylindrical in form by the mid-18th century, like the bottles of today. These could be stacked horizontally, to allow the wine to mature (known as binning) and to prevent the cork stopper from shrinking by keeping it in contact with the liquid.

Dark green wine bottles were among the first vessels to be produced in North America, and their manufacture remained an integral part of the nation's industry thereafter.

Miscellaneous bottles

In England, special glass bottles for foods and medicines were manufactured extensively from c.1850 onwards. An ingenious bottle for mineral water, designed with a glass marble stopper, was patented in 1858 (replacing earlier egg-shaped vessels) and the first milk bottle was patented in 1886. In America, bottles for health tonics, smelling salts and confectionery were produced throughout the 1800s, and coloured pictorial bottles (blown in full-size hinged moulds) enjoyed immense popularity with their low relief portraits of national celebrities and historical events (see Flasks).

During the 19th century, various steps were taken to mechanise the manufacture of bottles, but it was not until

Left Selection of carafes: the green-tinted one with a kick base is probably French, c. 1790; the small English carafes, made in sets of six to eight for the dining table, are similar in style to contemporary decanters of the period c. 1810–15 (4¾in).

Above right Rare Venetian *cristallo* carafe of unusual octagonal form, c. 1650. Only a handful of examples are known to exist.

Above Bohemian carafe and tumbler of overlay glass, cut with "windows", c. 1840.

1898 that the first entirely automatic bottle-making machine was invented by the American Michael Owens. Up to 2,500 bottles could be produced per hour by this process, which was rapidly adopted in Europe.

CARAFES

The term, probably derived from the Arabic *gharrāfah*, is used to describe a bottle for holding water or wine. Portable glass vessels for storing and serving liquid – including thinly blown bottles, jugs and flasks – have been made since Roman times. In England, carafes were made by Ravenscroft c. 1680, and during the 18th century, when they were known as "carrosts" or "crafts", they became important additions at the dining table. The carafe, filled with water or wine, was brought to the table for immediate use – hence the absence of a stopper, and the usual everted lip or spout to facilitate pouring. During the 18th century, English and Irish examples followed decanter styles (although carafes were generally smaller), with or without neck-rings and sometimes decorated with wheel-engraved pictorial and commemorative scenes – cut simply with flutes at the base – or with "brilliant" cutting after c. 1850.

127

SERVING DRINKS

By the late 19th century, carafes had declined in popularity, although they were sometimes placed in bedrooms, accompanied by a glass tumbler which could be inverted to rest over the neck of the bottle. Recently, the use of carafes at the dining table has again become common.

Similar bottles for serving water and wine (i.e. with no stopper and everted lip or spout) were made in many parts of Europe. In southern Spain, the *botijo*, a bottle with a spout for holding and pouring water, was produced widely from the 17th century onwards; it was made of earthenware or glass, the latter usually adorned with applied pincered threads. The factory of La Granja de San Ildefonso produced matching sets of water bottles and tumblers c. 1780, decorated with boldly coloured enamels. At the same time, water bottles with everted lips were being made in Murano; they were sometimes enamelled with pictorial scenes on opaque white glass. In Sweden, conical-shaped carafes were produced at the Skänska glass-house c. 1691–1762. And in Russia, crystal wine glasses and carafes were ordered by the imperial court during the mid-18th century. Onion-shaped carafes or *zirat flaske* were made during the early 1700s in Norway, with or without handles and decorated with pincered trails.

DECANTERS
The term "decanter" was first employed in England c. 1710 to describe a type of bottle for serving wine (and later, other drinks such as spirits, port and sherry) at the dining table. The liquid was previously canted, or tilted out, from its original bottle or container into the decanter so that it was free from sediment. Early types, known as serving or decanter bottles, appeared in dark-coloured soda glass

Right Mallet-shaped decanter with faceted pinnacle stopper, engraved with vines and Champagne label. English, c. 1765–75.

Below Popular decanter styles of different periods.
Left to right Ship's decanter with wide spreading base, triple-ringed neck and mushroom stopper, c. 1810; early decanter bottle with "nipt diamond waies" decoration, English or Dutch, c. 1680; cruciform decanter with mould-blown projecting side, c. 1740; dome-shaped with hollow stopper, c. 1880.

c. 1630 in "shaft and globe" form (see Bottles, p. 124), and c. 1677 in clear lead glass, with or without loose-fitting stoppers (indicating that the wine was consumed immediately). Late 17th and early 18th-century examples continued to reflect shaft and globe bottle designs (these persisted until c. 1750) or, alternatively, were designed as jugs with wide pouring spouts and handles (see Jugs). From c. 1730 decanters of numerous shapes were introduced, the majority of clear, fine quality metal.

Mallet-shaped. A pervasive type from c. 1740–80, initially of plain heavy glass with a kick base and occasionally a handle. After c. 1750 examples were less substantial (a result of the Glass Excise Acts) and handles and kicks disappeared.

Cruciform. Distinguished by their mould-blown projecting sides in the form of a cross, possibly meant to facilitate cooling of the wine, produced c. 1740–60. Early examples

Left Sulphide decanter with a cameo portrait of Sir Walter Scott, by John Ford and Co. of Edinburgh, c. 1840–50.

Far left English decanters of blue-tinted glass: the large quart size "Brandy" with gilded drink label, c. 1770; and the "Holland" and "Shrub" from a set of three, c. 1790. To differentiate between pairs, gilded numbers were sometimes placed on the bases of stoppers and decanters.

were made of thick metal and were designed with collared tops (the prototype of the neck-ring).

Shouldered. Designed with pronounced although downward-sloping shoulders and long ring-less necks, from c. 1745.

Ice decanters. The interiors of these curious pieces were fitted with a bladder-shaped container for storing ice; they were used for champagne or wine, and produced in limited numbers c. 1755–70.

Tapering. Of flowing elongated shape, in keeping with neo-classical tastes, c. 1770.

Barrel-shaped. Cut with flutes to simulate staves and hoops, c. 1780.

Ship's decanters. With outward-sloping sides and wide bases for greater stability at sea, produced from c. 1780.

After c. 1750, decanters were designed with close-fitting stoppers which were ground into the plain or ringed necks. In such airtight decanters drinks such as whisky or port (the latter becoming increasingly popular at this time) could be preserved indefinitely. Stoppers were as variously shaped as decanters: the spire or pinnacle stopper was first to appear (from c. 1750) followed by the disc, the mushroom (c. 1780–1825), the bull's-eye or target, and variations of these from c. 1810 onwards. Other stylistic changes included the gradual shortening and disappearance of the kick base by c. 1750 and the introduction of surface decoration. Clear, colourless examples were frequently cut with flutes at the base and facets around the shoulders, with further overall cutting on the body and stopper. Alternatively, decanters were enamelled or engraved with fruiting vine motifs and drink "labels" in imitation of silver-chained tags. From c. 1790 onwards, neck-rings became an established feature; they are usually of double or triple form, to provide a better grip. Coloured decanters were produced at Bristol and elsewhere from c. 1770, with drink names gilded on the body, and initialled stoppers. Throughout the 19th century, decanter styles remained varied – enamelled, engraved, deeply cut, or moulded to simulate hand-cut designs.

Above Cut glass decanter with triple-ringed neck and mushroom stopper, marked "Penrose Waterford", late 18th century.

Left Bohemian flask, enamelled with a cypher in an oval medallion, floral motifs and the date 1661. With pewter screw cap; 10½in.

Decanters were produced as single items, or in matching sets housed in wooden cases known as tantali. After c.1850, brightly coloured and flashed examples follow Bohemian styles, although plain Georgian decanters continued to be reproduced.

In Ireland, deeply cut and engraved decanters were manufactured extensively c.1780–1825, some with moulded bases impressed with vertical flutes and factory marks on the underside of the base. To compete with Anglo-Irish examples, North American decanters were blown into tripartite moulds ("blown-three-mould"), an inexpensive method used from c.1820 to create a variety of low-relief surface designs in imitation of hand-cutting. For a luxury market, hand-cut examples were also produced and after c.1860, several American decanters followed art glass styles.

A few decanter bottles were made at Venice and in Barcelona from the 16th century onwards, but it was not until the 18th century that their manufacture became widespread throughout Europe for luxury markets. At the Spanish factory La Granja de San Ildefonso, engraved and enamelled decanters were produced c.1775 modelled on contemporary English prototypes, and in Bohemia matching decanter sets were cut and engraved in neo-classical style around 1780. Throughout the 19th century, decanters of elaborate design were manufactured in France, Bohemia, Austria and at Venice.

FLASKS

Glass flasks have been manufactured in great variety since ancient times. The term describes either (i) a vessel for holding wines, spirits or other liquids for table use, variously shaped but characterised by a neck, mouth and usually a stopper, or (ii) a small, sometimes flat, bottle (up to 1 pint capacity) for holding wines and spirits and designed for travelling – i.e. kept in pockets or hung from the shoulder. (See also Decanters, previous pages.)

Lentoid flask. Of flattened globular shape with a cylindrical (sometimes flared) neck and rim, and two small loop handles extending from the mid-neck to shoulders. Small core-formed examples survive of opaque coloured glass of ancient Egyptian manufacture c.1400 BC, with a rounded base and no foot.

Barrel flask. A novelty table flask in the form of a barrel on its side, tapering at both ends with a short neck at the top, and mounted on four feet. Examples have been excavated in Rhineland regions, dating to the 2nd–3rd centuries AD. Others were made in Germany (*Fassflasche*), Venice, France and Spain (*barralets*) during the 17th and 18th centuries. The *barralets*, decorated with filigree threads and applied trails, were probably used for brandy.

Dropper flask. Variously shaped, but always with a small tube that projects outwards from the interior, used as a dropper; made throughout the Roman empire, 1st–4th centuries AD.

Gemel flask. Two flasks fused together, each blown separately and with separate neck and interior to contain different liquids (frequently used as a double cruet). There are examples made in Roman times, some of triple-neck form, and later gemel cruet flasks were made in Germany from the 17th century, in the U.S.A. c. 1800–1850, and in England in "Nailsea" glass c. 1790–1880.

Head flask. Mould-blown and decorated with a human mask on one or both (Janus flasks) sides of the body, below the neck. Some were grotesquely modelled, variously coloured and produced as amusing novelties during Roman times (1st–4th centuries AD). The form was later revived in Venice, Spain (Barcelona) and other parts of Europe.

Shell flask. Mould-blown and decorated with scallop shells below the neck; Roman (particularly Rhineland), 1st–3rd centuries AD, and revived in Venice c. 1500.

Helmet flask. A novelty type which, when inverted to stand on the splayed neck-rim, appears as a face and helmet; excavated in graves in Rhineland regions, 3rd–4th

Above Nailsea flasks, *left* in the form of a bellows decorated with pink combing on the opaque white body, *right* of double or "gemel" form in the filigree style. English, mid-19th century.

Right Quart-size historical flask of aquamarine glass, moulded in low relief with a hunter and the slogan "For Pike's Peak". American, 19th century.

Left Flasks of different shapes, including a Roman shell flask, c. 300 AD; pilgrim flask, Egypt or Syria, c. 1300; pistol flask, Saxony, dated 1596; barrel flask, Venetian, 18th century.

centuries AD, and probably used as a perfume-dropper.

Devotional flask. Rectangular or hexagonal, cold-painted or enamelled with a saint, and used to contain holy water. Examples were made in Venice and elsewhere in Europe, from c. 1600.

Pilgrim flask. A widespread type (appearing also in ceramics) known since Roman times, of flattened globular form, sometimes with small handles to hold a cord for hanging over shoulders (and originally used by pilgrims to contain water). Fine enamelled and gilded examples were made in Egypt and Syria c. 1250–1350, and later in Venice in the 1500s similarly decorated, sometimes with armorial motifs – probably for export to Germany.

Pistol flask. Of pistol-shape, usually with a metal stopper. Produced as an amusing novelty in Venice, Germany and Bohemia from the early 1600s; popular in the 19th century.

Pocket flask. Small and flat, carried in the hip pocket, for holding wines or spirits (occasionally with two separate necks and interiors), and fitted with a screw-top or stopper. Glass pocket flasks were made throughout Europe by the early 17th century (and in North America by c. 1765–70); they were made of thick glass and by c. 1700 were usually enclosed in leather or in wicker cases to prevent breakage.

Historical flask. Popular in the U.S.A. c. 1800–1880 for whisky and other spirits and mould blown with various historical scenes, portraits, slogans and landmarks shaped in low-relief. Most are of bottle glass, or brightly coloured (e.g. aquamarine).

JUGS

Glass jugs for holding and pouring liquids have been made since ancient times. Jugs may be characterised by a large loop handle, a pouring lip and bulbous-shaped body (globular, ovoid, baluster etc.), sometimes on a flared foot. Small core-formed examples of opaque coloured glass (called *oenochoë*) from the 15th–14th centuries BC have been found throughout the Near East; they were used to contain perfumed essences and oils. Roman blown jugs for oils and wines were of various sizes; many were of unrefined green glass, frequently mould-blown and un-adorned, although several types were coloured and moulded with symbolic motifs or appear marbled, mottled or bear snake-thread decoration. Jugs continued to be manufactured throughout the Islamic period, when they were often cut and engraved with geometric motifs and designed with pronounced beak spouts. In mediaeval forest glass-houses of Europe, thick green glass jugs were produced, and with the revival of fine glass-making in Venice from about 1450 jugs of artistic merit were designed and soon adopted in Europe. It is important to realise, however, that while luxury jugs and other objects were manufactured in glass from this period onwards, those for everyday use were usually made of other materials such as metal or pottery, and it was not until the middle to late 18th century that examples in glass were made for a wider market.

Ewer. A jug with a wide pouring lip, sometimes accompanied by a matching basin (i.e. for washing) and made in Venice from the early 1500s of *cristallo* metal with engraved or filigree decoration, or of marbled or *millefiori* glass. *Façon de Venise* ewers were made at Barcelona in the 16th and 17th centuries, and in Bohemia, Germany and Belgium, where they were enamelled with portraits and armorial motifs or bear twisted filigree patterns.

Decanter jug. Designed usually with a tall neck, lipped mouth and large loop handle, made in England and elsewhere from c.1670 and used to carry wine from the cask to the table where it was consumed immediately (many were designed with or without loose-fitting stoppers – see Decanters, p. 128). Early English specimens in soda

Opaline ewer and basin of "bulle de savon" (soap bubble) colour, mounted in ormolu. Probably Baccarat, c.1825; 12in.

glass have survived from the 1670s, and thereafter made of lead glass by Ravenscroft and others. During the late 18th century, decorative examples were made at La Granja de San Ildefonso, and in Germany a type with an interior pocket to contain ice, known as a *Kühlflasche*, was also produced.

Cántaro. A jug-cum-drinking vessel with two spouts – one for filling, the other for drinking – with a large circular handle on top and a decorative finial; made for wine throughout Catalonia from the 17th century, and in Venice (probably for export to Spain).

Claret jug. Made in England from the late 17th century and later in Ireland and elsewhere. Many followed the decorative surface designs of decanters (and were accompanied by decanter-type stoppers) and were of clear colourless lead glass, cut simply or, by c.1820, with elaborate overall cutting. Nineteenth-century claret jugs are frequently mounted in silver at the neck, spout and handle, some garishly decorated in revived baroque and rococo styles (c.1840–70) and later following the sinuous curves of Art Nouveau as it was adopted throughout Europe.

Water jug. For formal use at the dining table, manufactured in large numbers in England and Ireland c.1780–1820, usually of thick lead glass and sometimes made in sets with matching tumblers and trays. A type of water jug with a pouring spout and handle, resembling a tea-pot, was made in southern France from c.1700.

Cream and milk jugs. When tea became fashionable

Left Bohemian red glass claret jug, faceted and gilded on the stopper and body, c.1840–50.

Right Two-handled cream jug of clear lead glass, decorated with step-cutting on the sides. Anglo-Irish, c.1825–30.

SERVING DRINKS

about 1750, large services of silver and porcelain were designed for its consumption. Glass cream jugs were made in relatively small numbers, generally with a baluster-shaped body (about 3 in high), pouring lip and handle, on either a flat base, a domed foot or, more rarely, on three feet (following silver prototypes). In England, coloured and opaque white examples were made at Bristol and elsewhere c.1770–1800, or were of clear cut lead glass. In North America, cream and milk jugs or pitchers (those for milk about 7 in high) were made of clear and coloured glass, pattern-moulded or with applied lily-pad motifs, some cut and engraved to compete with Anglo-Irish imports.

PUNCH BOWLS, GLASSES AND FILLERS

Punch, introduced from India, was fashionable in England from c.1650; it was prepared in a large bowl about 10 inches in diameter from ingredients including a spirit such as brandy. The few glass examples which appeared before 1750 were modelled on metal and ceramic types – a large circular bowl, usually on a domed foot. From c.1780, clear colourless glass bowls were cut and engraved in characteristic Anglo-Irish styles, often accompanied by a matching ladle and a set of drinking glasses – initially of stemmed variety, but later superseded by small handled (stemless) cups during the early 1800s. Glass "toddy lifters" or "punch fillers" resembling miniature decanters about 6 inches high, but with a small opening at the top and base, were popular throughout Britain from c.1780 and eventually replaced ladles. The filler was dipped into the bowl, collecting a small

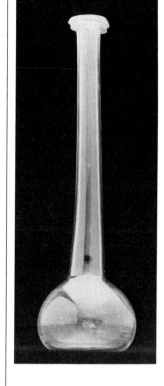

Above Clear glass toddy lifter, pierced with small holes at the top and bottom for transferring punch from the serving bowl to drinking glass. About 1800.

Left Punch bowl mounted on a flared foot, cut in "brilliant" style with geometric rosettes. By the Libbey Glass Co. of Toledo, Ohio, c.1902; 12$\frac{5}{8}$in high.

One of a pair of green-tinted
wine glass coolers, designed
with two lips. English, c. 1790.

Overleaf Fruit basket and
matching stand of clear
colourless glass, the sides
composed of an openwork
trellis adorned with applied
prunts. Probably Liège, 18th
century.

Below "Pittsburgh type" clear
lead glass pitcher, engraved
characteristically with daisies
and leafy sprays following the
traditions set by Stiegel during
the second half of the 18th
century. About 1820–35.

quantity of punch, and the top hole was covered by the
thumb; it could then be held over the drinking glass, and the
punch released. Fillers were often decoratively cut,
sometimes with a collar halfway up the neck to facilitate
holding.

Punch sets were also made in Bohemia, cut and engraved
with matching stemmed glasses, and in the U.S.A. after
c. 1830, coloured and pressed with decorative patterns or
heavily cut and sometimes flashed in "brilliant" style.

WINE GLASS COOLERS
During the late 17th century, large silver and ceramic bowls
with scalloped rims (for holding up to six glasses) known as
monteiths were produced in England and elsewhere –
"basons notched at the brim to let drinking glasses hang by
the foot". Glass monteiths in c. 1700 were rare, but smaller
glass versions or "coolers" holding up to two glasses, with
one or two lips at the rim, appeared during the early 18th
century, achieving their greatest popularity about
1750–1860. During this period, it was fashionable in
wealthy homes to provide each diner with a cooler filled
with iced water and pair of wine glasses. When the first
glass was empty, it was rinsed and chilled in the cooler
(suspended by the foot) while the second glass was
employed for the next wine. Late 18th-century examples

were frequently of "Bristol blue" and other coloured glass – plain or gilded with key-fret borders around the rim. Coolers were also made of clear lead glass in Ireland c. 1780–1820, cut and/or engraved, sometimes made in sets or as part of large dessert or wine services.

BASKETS

Of various sizes, designed with trailed and pincered threads built up around the sides to simulate wicker-work, often with a curved handle over the top. Baskets were intended for decorative display – or for holding fruit, cake, bread and sweetmeats. They were manufactured from the late 17th century onwards, particularly at places which specialised in the elaborate manipulation of a highly ductile glass, such as Venice. Here, the openwork trellis patterns which featured on baskets and other objects were referred to as *traforato* (perforated) and the style was imitated in the Low Countries (e.g. Liège), and in southern Spain.

In Britain, baskets were advertised only occasionally from c. 1725 (although small versions for holding sweetmeats and cakes were hung from *épergnes* after c. 1750). During the 19th century, however, decorative baskets, sometimes accompanied by matching tripod stands, were highly favoured; they were manufactured in England, Bohemia and America in clear cut glass, or following "art" styles. Others were press-moulded in "slag". Vaseline and brightly coloured opaque glass. Among American Art Nouveau designers who created a range of baskets during the early 1900s were Tiffany (in lustre glass with protruding mesh surrounds) and the Quezal Art Glass and Decorating Co. (with pulled-thread decoration and twisted "rope" handles).

BOWLS

Bowls have been manufactured for many purposes and in large numbers since ancient times. Many of Roman origin have survived of unrefined green glass, made in moulds and decorated with pronounced radiating ribs or "pillars" which protrude from the surface. Rarer Roman examples exist: of mosaic and marble glass, frequently adorned with twisted "rope" rims; mould-blown and coloured with decorative panels enclosing plant and animal motifs; of "gold sandwich glass" (i.e. gold or silver leaf sandwiched between two layers of transparent glass), enclosing a portrait medallion at the base, of which only fragments have survived; and wheel-cut with geometric and figural designs, found in graves throughout Europe and the Near East.

SERVING FOOD

With the revival of fine glass-making in Venice about 1450, many Roman styles were revived and bowls were again made of mosaic and *millefiori* glass. Most catered for luxury markets, and were designed for both decorative and utilitarian purposes. Notable types include standing bowls mounted on thick stems and flared feet, enamelled with geometric motifs (late 15th century); ice glass or filigree bowls of cylindrical form, designed with handles and matching covers surmounted by ornate finials, on three bun feet, probably for fruit and/or decoration (1500s onwards); and bowls of aventurine glass, and others in imitation of semi-precious stones (since the 1600s).

In England, glass bowls were imported from Venice during the 1660s and 1670s by the Glass Sellers' Company of London, and shortly thereafter examples were manufactured in the new lead glass by Ravenscroft and others. It was not until the 18th century, however, that examples were designated (both in England and abroad) for specific functions: for sweetmeats, goldfish, punch, fruit, salad, butter, sugar, cream, and for cleansing fingers ... "all sorts, the greatest variety ever seen" (as advertised during the period).

Sugar bowls. Made in Europe and North America from

Below Finger bowl of opaque white glass, gilded with festoons of husks and bucrania in the manner of James Giles, c.1775; 4¾in diameter.

Bottom Large 16th-century Venetian bowl, enamelled with a dotted feather pattern around the rim, and stag at the centre.

Above Rare Roman bowl of amber-coloured glass, cut cameo-style with white encircling bands in relief. Only three examples of this type are known to exist. Augustan period, late 1st century BC–1st century AD.

Right Small amethyst-tinted bowl with ribbed sides. English, c. 1800; 4in high.

SERVING FOOD

c. 1750, usually with covers, and sometimes *en suite* with a tea service or matching cream jug. European (e.g. Bohemian) types were often of opaque white glass (to imitate fine porcelain) while American examples were richly coloured and moulded.

Finger bowls. For cleansing the fingers at the dining table; thought to have evolved from the "water glass" of tumbler form which was used before c. 1750 for rinsing the mouth after eating (described as a filthy custom by one contemporary English writer). Between about 1760 and 1830, finger bowls or "washers" were widely manufactured, often in large matching sets. English examples were commonly decorated, of clear and coloured glass. Similar bowls with one or two lips at the rim are sometimes referred to today as finger bowls; it is more likely, however, that the majority were used to rinse and cool the bowls of wine glasses (see Wine Glass Coolers, p. 141) although it is possible that some lipped bowls served a dual purpose.

Fruit or salad bowls. Large bowls, probably intended for fruit, were manufactured extensively in Ireland and England c. 1780–1825. Most were boat-shaped or circular, with pronounced scalloped or turn-over rims. Early examples (c. 1750) were mounted on three feet in imitation of silver prototypes. By c. 1780, bowls were mounted on hollow or solid stands, usually made separately, the bases of which were moulded into circular, diamond or square shapes by the end of the century. Salad bowls were made of clear colourless glass, and mostly cut with sunburst motifs, lozenges and shell borders.

CRUETS AND CASTORS

These small bottles, usually with a stopper or lid and sometimes a handle, are for serving condiments (oil, vinegar, lemon juice, etc.) at the dining table. Cruets were imported into England from Venice during the 1660s and 1670s by the Glass Sellers' Company of London, and soon afterwards George Ravenscroft produced "diamond cruets", so called for their distinctive raised network decoration. By the 1690s, many cruets were silver-mounted and hallmarked (usually at the neck). Those made with stands – generally of silver, silver plate or wood – rarely show pontil marks, which were removed to prevent bottles from tilting or falling. Early forms were mallet-shaped and during the 1730s were characteristically diamond cut. Some, inscribed with the name of their contents, were made in sets consisting of four or more bottles including "castors" for dry condiments with perforated metal tops for sprinkling mustard, pepper, salt, etc. Between 1750 and 1785, cruets were commonly cut with facets over the neck and shoulders and new forms appeared: pear-shaped, cylindrical with

Condiment set of green-tinted glass consisting of six cruets, each gilded with contents' labels and geometric motifs on the pinnacle stoppers. The wooden stand is original. English, late 18th century.

tapering neck (c.1775), and urn-shaped on a spreading foot (c.1780) reflecting neo-classical tastes. Cut facets were now replaced by vertical flutes often intersected by encircling horizontal lines creating an elegant hooped effect. These styles were prevalent until c.1790, and examples can still be found with their original stands. Other late 18th- and early 19th-century cruets were of "Bristol blue", green or other richly coloured glass, frequently gilded with the name of their contents and usually consisting of oil and vinegar bottles and three castors, in Sheffield plate or wood stands. Opaque-white glass was also used for cruets from the mid-18th century, decorated with enamelling and made in south Staffordshire and elsewhere, while those of clear glass were engraved, gilded or cut in sharp relief.

The cruet was known in the Catalonian region of Spain as early as the 15th century. Called a *setrill*, it evolved as a distinctly national form with a circular body, tall thick neck, long curved spout and loop handle. Double cruets were also

147

Left Five cruet bottles of shouldered form, painted in coloured enamels with naturalistic flowers. All mounted in silver, complete with original lignum-vitae stand. Possibly London, c. 1760–65.

Right Milchglas mustard pot, enamelled in pastel shades with the portrait of a man, and gilded band around the rim. German, 18th century.

widely made (see "Gemel flask", p. 134). In France, a distinctive cruet was used for sacramental wine, the *burette*, characterised by an elongated curved spout and loop handle. A *porte-huilier*, or cruet-stand, was also designed for holding oil and vinegar bottles.

Variously coloured glass cruets were made in the U.S.A. during the 19th century: mould-blown with ribbing, cut with facets, and later, in "art" styles such as those of Satin glass.

JARS

Jars, with or without handles or covers, have been manufactured since ancient times to contain perfumed essences, toiletries, trinkets, even the ashes of the deceased, but more recently foods, preserves, relishes and medicines. One of the earliest surviving examples (in the British Museum) was made in ancient Egypt during the 18th Dynasty (c. 1440 BC), for holding ointments, of opaque turquoise glass with a matching lid.

Roman glass jars were frequently mould-blown of unrefined green or artificially coloured glass, some in

149

imitation of marble and natural stone. One covered type, known as a *pyxis*, was probably used to contain jewels and trinkets, while others with Christian and Jewish symbols, moulded in relief, may have contained holy water.

Tall covered jars (up to 20 inches high) were manufactured in Barcelona from the late 16th century. Some mould-blown examples, gilded and enamelled with the royal coat-of-arms, were made in 1794 for pharmaceutical use at La Granja de San Ildefonso for the Royal Palace at Madrid. A variety of enamelled jars were made in Germany and Bohemia during the 17th century, decorated with armorial motifs, secular subjects and biblical inscriptions; a few of these are mounted on three bun feet with flat matching lids. Some of opaque white glass were designed for mustard and other condiments during the 18th century. In England, exquisite opaque white covered jars decorated with naturalistically rendered floral bouquets were produced in sets, advertised in 1767 as ". . . neatly painted, the Colours more beautiful than China".

During the 19th century, a wider range of domestic jars appeared, some of dark blue and green glass with stoppers for holding medicines (the blue signifying that the content was poisonous), and other machine-made jars for holding beef extracts (e.g. Bovril) and other foods.

JELLY GLASSES
Made in England of various shapes and styles (most 4–5

Right *Heroes Recruiting at Kelsey's; Or Guard Day at St James's,* an engraving by the English caricaturist James Gillray. The officers neglect their duties for jellies and sugar plums at this famous fruiterer's in St James's Street. Note the jelly glasses and confectionary jars in the window. Dated June 9th, 1797.

Left Jelly glasses: *left* hexagonal, English, c. 1760; *centre* with ribbed surface patterning, English, c. 1770; *right* star-cut and mounted on an unusual foot with projecting sides (also found on contemporary salts and wine glasses), probably Irish c. 1780

Below Syllabub or custard glass with double-looped handles, set on a domed foot. English, c. 1730–50.

inches high) since the late 17th century, for serving portions of desserts such as jellies, creams and trifles. Early examples (c. 1680–1715) consist of a conical bowl with handles on both sides, stemless and mounted on a domed or spreading foot. Bell-shaped bowls, popular after c. 1710, were frequently pattern-moulded with diamond and ribbed designs (sometimes additionally adorned with applied threads) and single- or double-loop handles. After 1745, however, jelly glasses were smaller, lighter and without handles. Moulded patterns were replaced by cut and engraved designs on the bowls, rims (e.g. scalloped) and feet. A popular 18th-century presentation was on salvers or "pyramids" (see Sweetmeat Glasses, below).

Jelly glasses with cut designs have been produced in Germany and Bohemia since the early 1700s. Examples were also manufactured in the U.S.A., possibly c. 1784–95 by J. F. Amelung and by factories in the New England region, some of these being of tumbler shape.

SERVING FOOD

SYLLABUB GLASSES

These glasses for drinking syllabub (made from whipped cream, alcohol and spices), were produced in England from c. 1676 and later in the U.S.A. from about 1800. Early examples probably resembled posset pots, but after c. 1725 "whipt sillibub glasses" or "whips" (capacity 3–4 ounces) were designed with or without handles, and spoutless. Some were cut with decorative designs, a few said to have been engraved with an "S" on the bell-shaped bowl to distinguish them from jelly glasses of similar appearance.

COMPÔTIERS

Bowls (also called comports or preserves) for eating stewed fruit, often mounted on stemmed feet, sometimes with covers. Produced in the 19th century in Europe and the U.S.A. of clear and coloured glass.

SWEETMEAT GLASSES

Made in England from c. 1676 (and earlier in silver and ceramic), and used for serving desserts such as candied fruits, nuts and chocolates. Eighteenth-century examples, sometimes advertised as dessert glasses, were $6\frac{1}{2}$–7 inches high and of various forms and styles but frequently consisted of a double-ogee bowl mounted on a tall stem (most popularly the mould-blown Silesian stem c. 1715–65, followed by the cut-facet c. 1770–1810). Bowls were sometimes pattern-moulded with diamond or

English sweetmeat glasses, *left* c. 1730; *right* cut profusely on the scalloped rim, bowl and faceted stem, c. 1770.

Left Silesian sweetmeat glass of shell shape; c. 1765.

Right Pyramid of four salvers set on Silesian stems and high domed feet, for holding jelly glasses and a sweetmeat at the top. English, c. 1750; overall height 30½in.

ribbed designs, echoed below on the feet which were domed, or domed and folded (to prevent chipping). Shallow cut motifs and scalloped rims were introduced after c. 1730, later becoming more elaborate and deeply incised in Anglo–Irish styles.

During the mid-18th century, it was fashionable to place a large sweetmeat glass on top of a pyramid of salvers, surrounded by various jelly glasses; alternatively, sweetmeats were served in baskets from *épergnes* (the latter presentation most popular from c. 1760 onwards).

Tall-stemmed dessert glasses, with wavy or shell-shaped bowls, had been manufactured in Venice since the 16th century, and imitated widely *à la façon de Venise*. Finely engraved examples, in rococo styles, were made in Germany, Silesia and Bohemia for export markets, c. 1730–60.

COMFIT GLASSES

Small sweetmeat glasses about 3–4 inches high, with or without a short stem. Eighteenth-century English examples were plain, or sometimes adorned with applied glass threads, moulded prunts and other motifs.

SALVERS AND OTHER DESSERT STANDS

The salver consisted of a circular plate mounted on a stemmed foot (4–8 inches high), manufactured in England c. 1680–1820 (and in Ireland after c. 1750), used for serving all kinds of wet and dry sweetmeats, coloured jellies, creams, etc. Like other English glassware, many were exported. Salvers were frequently tiered into pyramids up to 30 inches high, with three or four of diminishing size one upon the other. The top salver invariably featured a large sweetmeat glass for holding dry confections, encircled by four to eight jelly glasses. Pyramids gradually declined in popularity from c. 1770 (probably superseded by the fashionable and more stable *épergnes*). After c. 1830, individual salvers were used as cake-stands in England and France. Tiered dessert stands known as *alzata* ("elevated"), each made of several pieces, were however produced in Venice throughout the 19th century.

SALTS

Small receptacles for holding salt at the dining table, on a flat base or stemmed foot. Glass salts were not manufactured extensively before c. 1700 in Europe and c. 1772 in the U.S.A., although metal salts had been known since mediaeval times, when they were larger for communal use. In England c. 1720–50, small glass salts for individual servings were modelled directly on silver prototypes, often about $2\frac{1}{2}$ inches high with a circular bowl mounted on three

Above Clear glass salts, the oblong pair cut profusely with diamonds, English c. 1800–10; the boat-shaped pair in the style of contemporary fruit bowls, Anglo-Irish c. 1790.

Below English salt, the circular body supported on three short applied feet with lions' paws and masks; early 1700s.

cabriole legs, each moulded with a lion's head or mask at the top and a paw foot. Thereafter, styles become increasingly diverse: round, oblong or boat-shaped, with extensive decorative cutting. In Ireland, salts resembled miniature fruit or salad bowls c. 1780–1825, with pronounced scalloped or turn-over rims, mounted on stemmed and moulded square feet.

In southern Spain, bowl-shaped salts on stemmed feet were made of unrefined green glass throughout the 18th century, characteristically decorated with applied pincered threads. At La Granja de San Ildefonso, fine crystal glass salts with gilded, enamelled and cut designs were produced c. 1775–85 for luxury and export markets, sometimes *en suite* with large dinner services. Other fine salts were made at this time in Venice, Bohemia and France. In the U.S.A., the introduction of mould-pressing c. 1827 led to the mass-production of salts in a wide and imaginative range of styles and colours.

SERVING FOOD

Left Façon de Venise charger in the *vetro a reticello* filigree style, with swirling opaque threads radiating from the shallow well. 17th century; 22⅔in diameter.

Below Pair of wafer stands, the shallow bowls decorated with stylised posies and applied spiralling threads around the rims, set on faceted baluster stems and circular star-cut feet. By the Saint-Louis factory, 19th century; 4¼in high.

Above A cut glass tea box with period ormolu mounts, French, c. 1820.

Above Staffordshire enamelled tea bottle of canted rectangular section, inscribed "Green" and painted with a goldfinch perched on a branch, with floral bouquets on the sides. The gilt-metal top is surmounted by an enamelled glass plaque. About 1760; 5½in.

PLATES AND DISHES

Made popularly of pressed glass in the U.S.A. and England after c. 1830, prior to which only small numbers were produced, a few dating to the 3rd century BC. Plates were usually designed with a central depression and surrounding outer rim, of circular or oval shape. Venetian plates date from the 1500s onwards (and *à la façon de Venise* in Barcelona, Antwerp and elsewhere). They are enamelled, gilded, diamond-point engraved or of filigree glass. Fine opaque white plates were also made at Murano c. 1740, painted in red to depict famous Venetian views, after etchings by Luca Carlevaris and Canaletto. They are attributed to the Miotti glass-houses.

TAZZE

The Italian word for cup, *"tazza"*, is commonly employed to describe a shallow standing dish, possibly intended originally for holding fruit and/or for decorative display. Many *tazze* were manufactured in Venice from c. 1500, mounted on stems of baluster shape, or moulded with masks and entwined glass threads. They followed filigree styles, and were sometimes also enamelled, gilded or engraved. *Tazze à la façon de Venise* were produced in Spain and the Low Countries.

TEA CADDIES

These boxes and bottles (about 5½ inches high) were made in glass in England from c. 1750–1820. The term caddy was derived from the Malay word *kati* for the standard weight (about 1¼ pounds) of tea, packed and exported from the Orient.

English tea bottles (also called canisters) were commonly of "Bristol blue" or opaque white glass, gilded and enamelled with floral scrolls and birds, and labelled with the brand of tea: Bohea, Green, Black and Hyson. Many were of rectangular section, with canted corners and silver or gold tops, sometimes also surmounted by an enamelled plaque. The majority have been ascribed traditionally to the Bristol area (particularly to the decorator Michael Edkins who worked here c. 1765), but it is more likely that they were of wider manufacture including Dublin, Sunderland, Warrington and the south Staffordshire area c. 1755–70, and that the surface designs were executed by numerous competent painters. Tea bottles were commonly made in pairs or sets.

Square and rectangular boxes with hinged metal lids were produced in clear and coloured glass, cut with large stars and flutes after c. 1765. A few clear and opaline glass caddies were also manufactured in France, mounted in ormolu and elaborately cut.

THE DESK

DESK ACCESSORIES

Glass desk sets, including paperknives, seals, pens and writer's companions, were made for an exclusive market from c. 1835. In Venice, the workshops of Franchini, Bigaglia and others produced desk sets of *millefiori* glass (coinciding with the popular revival of the technique c. 1840) with implements mounted in silver-gilt. The *millefiori* was often studded with minute canes displaying portraits, gondalas and famous Venetian views, sometimes with dates and initials (perhaps those of the purchaser), catering largely to the tourist trade. In France, factories such as Clichy, Baccarat and Saint-Louis renowned for their paperweights also manufactured small seals, inkwells and other accessories, similarly decorated with *millefiori* canes and floral bouquets enclosed within clear glass. Later, large desk sets were mass-produced by Lalique c. 1918–30, of clear and coloured glass, including objects such as ashtrays, pintrays, picture frames, blotters, seals, etc. in a wide and imaginative range of styles, catering to luxury markets throughout Europe and America.

Below Millefiori glass desk accessories including a writer's companion mounted in filigree silver and dated 1847 on a single cane; a plaque dated 1846, with aventurine inclusions; a cane handle dated 1845; and a paper-knife with gilt-metal blade dated 1847 (8⅜in long). Some pieces possibly made by the Franchini workshop.

Below right Stourbridge inkwell with paperweight stopper and base in *millefiori* style, c. 1850.

Right Cut glass inkwell mounted in silver, with detachable glass well, hallmarked London 1827.

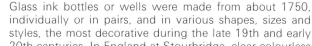

INK BOTTLES AND STANDS

Glass ink bottles or wells were made from about 1750, individually or in pairs, and in various shapes, sizes and styles, the most decorative during the late 19th and early 20th centuries. In England at Stourbridge, clear colourless examples, 6–7 inches high, were made with *millefiori* discs at the base and stopper c. 1840–60; others were cut, moulded or pressed, with silver or Sheffield plate on the stopper or lid and a matching stand. Similar pieces made in France often have bronze and ormolu mounts. In the U.S.A., small cylindrical ink bottles were made c. 1825, of olive or amber bottle glass (seldom colourless, or brightly coloured) decorated in low relief and manufactured at factories in New Hampshire, Connecticut and Massachusetts. Later, art glass styles were popular, such as the iridescent and silver-mounted ink bottles by Tiffany, c. 1905. In France, many were designed in the Art Nouveau and Art Deco styles (e.g. of cameo glass by Daum, c. 1900) and mass-produced for luxury markets by Lalique in the 1920s and 1930s (see Desk Accessories).

Ink-stands were rarely made of glass (metal and wood being preferred) but several were designed by Lalique to contain two inkwells.

Left to right, above A Saint-Louis carpet-ground weight with green, pink and white canes ($2\frac{1}{4}$in diameter); a Clichy overlay weight, the outermost blue layer cut through with "windows" to reveal close-*millefiori* canes; a Saint-Louis "pom-pon" weight, the white flower on a swirling pink, blue and white ground. *Below* Pink *millefiori* carpet-ground weight, the central composite cane surrounded by five silhouette canes, by Saint-Louis ($2\frac{1}{2}$in diameter); Clichy overlay weight, with concentric *millefiori*; a Baccarat double-clematis and garland weight. All c. 1850.

Bottom left On the *left* a rare moulded salamander weight, the globular jasper-ground base surmounted by a gilt reptile, by Saint-Louis. *Right* snake weight of facet-cut glass, enclosing a pink and green coiled serpent on a white filigree ground, Saint-Louis; $3\frac{1}{16}$in.

Bottom right Victorian glass door-stop, the interior decorated with tiered flowers in a pot. Midlands, c. 1870; $3\frac{3}{4}$in.

PAPERWEIGHTS

These highly decorative objects, usually spherical, solid and heavy, for holding down papers on a desk, were made in large numbers by factories in France, Bohemia, Belgium, Britain, the U.S.A, China and Japan. Their introduction is attributed to the Venetian glass-maker Pietro Bigaglia, who exhibited *millefiori* weights in Vienna in 1845.

The finest paperweights were made entirely by hand (as they are today), in an unlimited range of styles. They are usually $2\frac{1}{2}$–3 inches in diameter, but there are also magnums (about 4 inches) and miniatures (about 2 inches). There are three main types of paperweight – sulphides, *millefiori* and "subjects", which are described below. A survey of the chief centres of manufacture follows on pp. 164–5.

Sulphides. Ceramic cameo medallions, mostly depicting famous figures and portraits, made in limited numbers by factories in France, England, the U.S.A., Germany and Bohemia. Sulphides were placed on clear or coloured grounds, sometimes combined with concentric circles of *millefiori*, and embedded in clear glass.

Millefiori. The most common type of weight, produced by the majority of factories and appearing in various styles: "close *millefiori*": the multi-coloured canes are placed tightly together over the whole ground, appearing in profile as an upright mushroom (i.e. high dome-shape) or a flattened disc; "spaced *millefiori*": the individual canes are separated at regular intervals or randomly, and placed on lacy or coloured grounds; "concentric *millefiori*": a popular design in which individual canes are arranged in circles; "panelled *millefiori*": canes are placed into clusters, each group separated by thick threads or canes of a distinctive appearance; "garlands": canes looped and interwoven into formal patterns; "carpets": tiny canes of the same colour and type packed tightly together; "swirls": two (rarely three) coloured rods are embedded and swirled into striped patterns, and adorned with a large central *millefiori* cane.

Subjects. Paperweights in which one (or more) flower, bouquet, fruit, bird, insect, reptile or animal is placed on a clear, coloured or mottled ground, sometimes combined with a *millefiori* or twisted ribbon surround, and embedded in clear glass. The subject was usually made at the lamp.

The exteriors of weights are often cut decoratively, with a large star or other motif on the underside of the base, which becomes magnified through the thick clear glass and forms part of the overall design. If the weight is cased or overlaid in one or more colours (almost invariably with an underlying layer of opaque white), it is cut with "windows" around the sides and on top which open onto the interior. Clear weights were sometimes faceted.

Left to right, top Dahlia head by Saint-Louis; modern parrot weight by Paul Ysart; rare Clichy weight with three-colour swirl design. *Centre* Modern Baccarat weight on sapphire ground; flower bouquet by Clichy; rare Baccarat weight with intricate *millefiori* design. *Bottom row* Bouquet with a pansy, by Baccarat; modern weight by Perthshire Paperweights Ltd, the Tudor rose surrounded by eight *millefiori* canes; Saint-Louis "crown" weight, hollow-blown and decorated with twisted ribbons. All antique weights c. 1850.

THE DESK

Manufacturers
France. Paperweights of the highest quality were produced in France by three firms. At Baccarat, the weights, made 1846–80, are renowned for their use of richly coloured motifs. Many pieces are initialled "B" on a single cane and some bear a date from the years 1846–53 (production resumed in 1952). Paperweights from Clichy (1846–c. 1870) won several prizes during the 1850s for excellence, and were acclaimed for their use of coloured overlays and the clarity of metal. Clichy weights are occasionally marked "C" or "CL" on a single cane (rarely the whole name), and are not dated. Saint-Louis manufactured 1845–c. 1850 a great variety of weights in a brief time. Examples are sometimes initalled "SL" or dated on a single cane. Production of weights resumed at Saint-Louis in the 1950s. The less well-known Paris factory of La Villette Pantin made attractive sulphide weights after c. 1850.

Bohemia. *Millefiori* weights were produced by various factories after c. 1845. One distinctive type, painted with flowers and classical scenes on the base or exterior (and unusually light in weight) is also thought to be of Bohemian or Silesian manufacture.

Belgium. The glassworks Val-Saint-Lambert has since c. 1850 produced *millefiori*, overlay and cut weights of fine quality. Hallmarks of the early style are the inclusion of a spiralling circle of coloured threads ("torsade") to frame the central motif and a flat un-cut base.

England. Numerous *millefiori* and "picture-postcard" weights were made as novelties from c. 1850, and sold at stationery shops. Finer weights were made in London at the Falcon Glassworks managed by Apsley Pellatt and famous for their sulphide weights; William Kidd; Rice, Harris and Co. (or the Islington Glassworks), examples sometimes initialled "IGW"; Whitefriars, some pieces dated between 1848 and 1853 (production resumed in 1953). In Birmingham George Bacchus and Sons made fine quality weights in a range of styles after c. 1848 and other examples were made by F. & C. Osler. Prominent among the numerous factories at Stourbridge which made paperweights was W. H. B. & J. Richardson.

In addition, large, heavy green glass weights or "doorstops" were made by bottle manufacturers throughout the country from c. 1830. Often decorated with air bubbles or tiered flowers inside, they are occasionally marked with the manufacturer's name.

Scotland. Fine weights are made today by Caithness Glass, many in abstract designs by Colin Terris; Perthshire Paperweights, often in limited editions of 500 to 3,000; and Paul Ysart, an independent designer of weights since 1971, all signed "PY" and largely exported to America.

U.S.A. Weights were made from c. 1853 (after international exhibitions held in London and New York), many based on European, especially French, prototypes. The New England Glass Co. produced fine overlay and cut examples, frequently with floral bouquets and fruit, including weights blown into the shape of a pear or apple. The Boston and Sandwich Glass Co. made *millefiori* and flower weights, including the well-known poinsettia. The Mount Washington Glass Co. specialised in large pink and red roses, dahlias and fruit, sometimes in magnum size. Whitall, Tatum & Co. (Millville, New Jersey) produced c. 1863–1918 distinctive upright weights (mostly flowers) including the well-known and naturalistically rendered "Millville rose" created by Ralph Barber. Many weights are mounted on pedestal stems. The Union Glass Co. (Somerville, Massachusetts) made cruder weights with miniature farm animals, placed on multi-coloured mottled grounds. Tiffany manufactured a few large and heavy weights in the early 1900s, some displaying aquatic life in aquamarine-coloured glass, and signed on the base. Bronze and lustre glass weights were also made c. 1913. Steuben made fine flower weights before the 1940s, some marked "Steuben" with a fleur-de-lis etched on or near the base.

China and Japan. Small (about 2 inches diameter) decorative weights have been made since c. 1930, usually with floral motifs and occasionally a green frog. Examples are of soda glass, hence light in weight and with a distinctive oily texture, and lack the clarity of fine French weights.

CANDLESTICKS

Glass candlesticks were produced in England, Venice, Germany, France and Spain from the 1600s onwards, and later in Ireland and (by c. 1760) in the U.S.A. Many glass candlesticks followed the designs of their metal prototypes (indeed metals continued to be preferred to glass), although those of Venetian and Spanish origin, for example, were characteristically adorned with applied and pincered trails, entwined threads, flowers and fantastic forms in keeping with national glass styles.

In England, glass candlesticks were modelled c. 1681–1715 closely on those of brass and silver. The standard design consisted of a nozzle or socket (for securing the wax candle), a tall column or shaft, a foot (usually domed and spreading, for stability) and frequently a grease-pan (underneath and encircling the nozzle to catch drips). Some candlesticks featured baluster motifs on the shaft like those found on contemporary brass candlesticks and wine glasses, and after c. 1714 the columns

continued to reflect fashionable styles of wine glass stem, usually with a greater number of knops and motifs (e.g. "true" and "inverted" balusters combined) to fill up the comparatively large expanse of the shaft. Among these styles are Silesian stems and variations of these c. 1714–50; filigree stems, briefly popular from c. 1740 onwards, particularly air-twists; and facet-cut stems from c. 1740, when decorative cutting extended to the whole of the surface, effectively dispersing the candlelight and creating an added brilliance. Neo-classical motifs were adopted c. 1775–95, e.g. urn-shaped or columnar shafts, taller (up to 15 inches high) and more elegant than before. The majority of 18th-century glass candlesticks were of clear and colourless metal, but a few of blue and opaque white were manufactured c. 1760–1800, probably at London and Midlands factories. All these types were adopted by glass-makers outside England. By the late 18th century, it became fashionable to decorate candlesticks with cut glass lustres, usually hung in fringes around the exteriors of grease-pans. After c. 1800, cutting became increasingly lavish.

In North America, glass candlesticks were produced in relatively small numbers (metal being preferred) and in a restricted range of styles. Characteristic late 18th-century types consisted of a long socket mounted on a domed saucer base (no shaft), pattern-moulded with an overall

English clear glass candlesticks, showing the progression of 18th century stem styles following those for wine glasses: true baluster stem, c. 1730 (*left*); Silesian stem, c. 1750 (*centre*); and unusually thin facet-cut stem, c. 1770.

Pair of candlesticks with cut glass pans and nozzles, mounted on ormolu and opaque white glass stands gilded with scrolls and a diaper pattern. Festoons of yellow glass drops hang from the grease-pans. London, probably the workshop of James Giles, c. 1775–80; 12in.

ribbed design; this style was reproduced commonly during the 19th century. A variation of this had a long socket drawn out to a hollow knopped shaft (i.e. made from a single gather of glass), mounted on an applied domed foot. Pressed candlesticks, in various colours and styles, were mass-produced from c. 1830. Some featured a large dolphin-shaped shaft, mounted on a thick square or multi-sided base.

CANDELABRA
Branched candle-holders for table use, with two or more arms for candle sockets, were made commonly of glass c. 1760–1880 in England. Originally advertised as "girandoles", they were called candelabra from c. 1792. Early examples (about 12 inches high) were plain, but after c. 1765 cutting became increasingly lavish, and the piece might be adorned with star or crescent finials at the top. After c. 1775, many were decorated with pendant drops, or lustres, which continued to feature on 19th-century candelabra. Examples mounted on jasper ware or ormolu stands, in neo-classical styles, were taller, up to 30 inches high.

Elaborate candelabra were made at notable French factories (e.g. Saint-Louis) throughout the 19th century; exported widely, they catered exclusively to the wealthy.

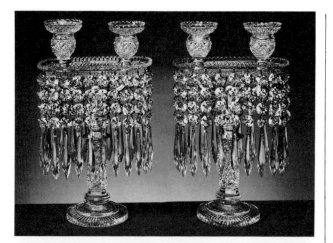

Left Pair of Regency candelabra of clear cut glass, decorated with a fringe of faceted pendant drops and "icicles" which hang from the sides of the grease-pans, nearly obscuring the arms and shaft. London, c. 1815.

Below Unusual cut glass candelabrum-cum-centrepiece, decorated with festoons of pendant drops. English, 18th century.

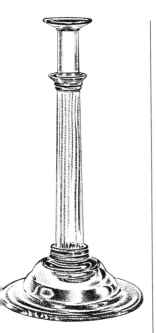

TAPERSTICKS

Small candlesticks (4–6 inches high) for holding tapers to light candles and pipes. In England c. 1740 they were sometimes referred to as tea-candlesticks and possibly intended for use on tea-tables. Tapersticks invariably followed the forms and styles of larger candlesticks.

WALL LIGHTS AND SCONCES

Manufactured in Venice since the early 1600s (and shortly thereafter in England), wall lights made of glass, or glass combined with metal, giltwood or ceramic, have one or more branches for holding candles. One type was designed with a light-reflecting back-plate, usually of polished metal or mirror glass (the latter employed by the late 17th century), called a sconce by c. 1712.

Venetian wall lights are most elaborate, composed of both clear and coloured glass, decorated with applied fruits, leaves and flowers (following the styles of contemporary

Above English taperstick, the hollow fluted shaft mounted on a domed and terraced foot; c. 1750.

Right One of a pair of Victorian wall brackets of clear cut glass, the three grease-pans supporting fringes of faceted pendant drops. About 1840.

chandeliers), and increasingly flamboyant during the 19th century. English examples are of more restrained appearance. One type (c. 1700) consists of a shaped mirror-glass plaque, bevelled and wheel-engraved with floral motifs, and fitted with a single metal branch and candle-socket. Later examples display pendant drops and cut surfaces in keeping with chandeliers of the period. In Ireland, distinctive wall lights were made from the late 18th century consisting of an oval mirror-glass back-plate framed by clear and blue glass segments (rarely, green) fitted with a metal hook on top from which a miniature chandelier was suspended.

Ornate and novelty wall lights continued to be produced during the Art Nouveau and Art Deco periods.

CHANDELIERS

Glass chandeliers have been made in Venice since the 18th century, and also in Britain, France, Spain and Bohemia, and in the U.S.A. following Art Nouveau styles from c. 1900. The chandelier consists basically of a central column or shaft from which numerous arms or branches project, each with a socket and grease-pan for a single candle (later adapted for gas and electric fittings during the 19th and early 20th centuries). This standard framework inspired by metal prototypes was adopted widely throughout Europe, and resulted in the appearance of several distinctive and readily identifiable types.

The finest Venetian glass chandeliers were characteristically composed of both clear and coloured glass and richly adorned with an array of naturalistic motifs, including flowers, leaves and fruits (examples can be seen at the Museo Vetrario in Murano). The ornaments were made individually at the lamp and subsequently attached to the glass or metal framework. Known as *ciocche* ("bouquet of flowers"), this style of chandelier has been reproduced with little variation since the time of its introduction, and exported widely throughout Europe. The 18th-century glass-maker Giuseppe Briati (d. 1772) was famous for the manufacture of fine and elaborate *ciocche* (some up to eight feet in diameter), and such pieces epitomise the splendour and extravagance of Venetian design.

In England, glass chandeliers were produced commonly after c. 1725. Early examples are plain and of simple construction, following brass prototypes. The shaft consists of a series of globular shapes, with a bowl at the base to which several curved arms are attached. Cutting – if it appears at all – is restrained and shallow, confined exclusively to the shaft. By c. 1745, however, styles became increasingly elaborate, and shallow cutting now extended over the whole – including the sockets, grease-pans and

Irish cut glass wall light hanging from a hook at the top of a mirror back plate, and framed by a border of faceted triangular pieces of alternately green and clear glass. This colour combination is exceptionally rare. About 1790; 28in.

Large ceiling chandelier decorated overall with coloured glass flowers and pincered trails of blue and pink. Attributed to the Venetian workshop of Giuseppe Briati, c. 1750.

branches – in diamond and star-shaped patterns. Shortly after this time, cut glass pendant drops were introduced and applied to the framework – initially in small numbers (so that the overall appearance was harmonious and uncluttered, no feature more prominent than the next), but by c. 1770 in greater profusion. Chandeliers followed rococo, then neo-classical styles, with extensive and sophisticated cutting, and under the influence of the architect-designers Robert and James Adam featured urn-shaped shafts (now elongated and elegant) and pear-shaped drops wired into chains and hung between the branches in swags, each pendant faceted in meticulous detail. By 1800, decorative ornaments had become so profuse that the underlying structure of the chandelier – the shaft and branches – was nearly obscured from view. During the Regency period (c. 1810–20), pendant "icicle" drops featured over the whole of the chandelier, hung in tiered curtains from top to

LIGHTING

Left Regency chandelier for six lights, hung with "rule cut" crystal drops over the whole. English, c.1820.

Right Small chandelier of moulded glass, the globular shaft and bowl supporting arms and decorated with festoons of pendant drops in the late 18th-century style. Manufactured by Perry and Co. of London, c.1850.

Below Large hall lantern, the clear glass sides mounted in lacquered brass with rich castings on the top crest and sides. English, c.1800.

Below right Table lamp decorated on the base in the *dolce relievo* ("soft relief") cameo style, with elephant-trunk motifs and classical figures in delicate shades of mauve and ivory. This technique was adopted exclusively by the English firm of Stevens and Williams (although few examples were signed), c.1870.

bottom, creating an effect not unlike a cascading waterfall. The arms and shaft were now completely hidden, and therefore usually undecorated. Many of these styles were reproduced, for either candle or gas, during the Victorian period with only slight variations in the cut decoration. The advent of electricity, however, brought about several changes in the styles of chandeliers, which now incorporated large areas of metal, and of course light bulbs, which were difficult to display aesthetically.

The greatest producers of chandeliers were, however, Germany and Bohemia, with a large export trade, from c.1720 to this day. The earliest examples are branch chandeliers, followed by the neo-classical "corona", in which a horizontal brass circle is hung with long glass drops. The French made elegant brass chandeliers of lyre shape, hung with finely cut pendants, also produced today.

Fine chandeliers were produced at the Spanish factory La Granja de San Ildefonso from c.1763, several commissioned by King Charles III for the royal palace. Few early examples have survived, but those manufactured later reflect the influence of contemporary English styles, some being decorated with pendant drops and "icicles" linked into chains, or tiered curtains in with Regency tastes.

Art Nouveau chandeliers (see also the following Lanterns and Lamps) introduced new shapes and styles from c. 1890, with a wider range of colours, pictorial motifs and decorative metal supports and frames. Examples were produced by leading designers in France (e.g. Gallé and Daum) and in the U.S.A. (e.g. Tiffany). Later, René Lalique created several types of chandelier in "traditional" and Art Deco styles.

LANTERNS AND LAMPS

Among the oldest and most celebrated glass lanterns surviving are the so-called mosque lamps produced in the Near East, particularly Syria, in large numbers and of fine quality during the 13th and 14th centuries. Exquisitely enamelled and gilded with quotations from the Koran in flowing calligraphy, these lanterns were suspended from the ceilings of mosques, secured by chains looped through the small side-handles. They were imitated in Venice for export to the Near East during the 15th and 16th centuries.

Lanterns of square or octagonal shape were also known in mediaeval Europe. These "lanthorns" – so called because the sides were composed of horn and other materials to protect the flame – were for lighting outside passages and draughty interiors. Glass lanterns were not produced before about 1650 in, for example, England. Usually incorporating metal frames and hooks, they initially had panes of pale green "window" glass; after c. 1676 the finest examples were fitted with lead glass plates ground, polished and sometimes decorated with wheel-engraving, a style popular in Bohemia and Germany. Lanterns featured commonly in the hallways of wealthy 18th-century homes.

Glass table lamps were made widely from the late 1600s onwards (in America, few examples can be dated before c. 1790). In Spain, free-blown oil lamps were produced commonly of unrefined green glass decorated with opaque white stripes, or brightly coloured and adorned with applied threads. They were designed with one or more "spouts" for containing wicks – placed near the base of the vessel (when hung), or alternatively at the top, resembling a candelabrum. Small portable types were also produced, with a large loop handle and elongated spout, mounted on a short stem and wide circular base. English oil lamps from c. 1680 were similarly constructed, with a globular resevoir or font (the interior of which was filled with oil for floating the wick), mounted on a stemmed foot, and usually with a loop handle. The majority were undecorated, clear and colourless. In the 18th century, few lighting improvements occurred until the invention, in 1784, of the Argand lamp. This new type, manufactured later by factories throughout Europe, was fitted with a glass tube and tubular wick, which

LIGHTING

permitted better air flow for feeding the flame and, hence, increased illumination. It was shortly (1798) improved upon by the Carcel lamp and the Moderator (1836 – this maintained a steady flow of oil to the wick), followed by further advances in the quality and refinement of oil and intensity of the flame. By the 1860s, numerous glass lamp patents had been issued and a wider range of decorative styles appeared in Europe and America – clear and coloured, with "frosted", cased and engraved shades and bases, or following "art" glass styles such as Queen's Burmese, Satin and Peachblow.

The advent of electricity (first bulb produced 1879), combined with the spirit of Art Nouveau, caused a sensation in lamp design. Glass and metal were blended together into breathtaking and spectacular forms – bases in the form of trees, figures or flowers, echoed by fragments of brilliantly coloured glass arranged into pictorial compositions on the shades, creating a stained glass effect. Lamps in this style were manufactured widely in the U.S.A. about 1890–1920, notably by Tiffany, and in Europe by designers such as Gallé, Daum and Müller in France, and Loetz in Austria. During the 1920s and 1930s, novelty lamps in Art Deco styles included those made by Lalique resembling giant scent bottles (*grandes veilleuses*) or as large panels incorporated into architectural schemes.

Above Victorian clear glass oil lamps, which still retain their original fonts. About 1850–60.

Right Glass lamp in the Art Deco style, decorated with geometric bands on the blue coloured base, echoed above on the white shade. With engraved signature "DAUM NANCY FRANCE", c. 1925.

174

FOR DECORATION

ARMORIAL AND MASONIC WARES

Coats-of-arms, heraldic shields, masonic emblems and inscriptions have appeared on European glass since the 16th century. Examples of earlier date are rare, but a few 13th-century specimens of Islamic design have survived, including the well-known "Aldrevandini" beaker (in the British Museum) enamelled with Swabian coats-of-arms and heraldic motifs such as stags' horns, possibly made in Venice during the 14th century.

Polychrome enamelled armorial wares – flasks, *tazze* and cups – were produced in Venice during the 16th century for the Italian aristocracy, and for export to Europe and the Near East. Armorial glassware of south German and Bohemian manufacture had appeared by c. 1550, and for the next 150 years an enormous range of armorial and masonic motifs were enamelled on *Humpen*, beakers, dishes, goblets and bottles and, more commonly, engraved on the heavier and more brilliant "potash" glass by the late 17th century. The arms of royal, imperial and ducal families were employed continuously to decorate the surfaces of vessels, the work executed by small local factories who catered exclusively to the courts and the wealthy. Corporations, guilds, towns, trades and crafts were also represented. Perhaps the most elaborate and impressive pieces are the brightly enamelled *Reichsadler* glasses depicting the double-headed eagle of the Holy Roman Empire, with its fierce eyes and open beaks. The breast was painted initially with a crucifix (the earliest surviving example, in the British Museum, is dated 1571) but this was shortly replaced with the orb of the state (the emperor's secular symbol) or with a portrait of Leopold I. The wings were covered with the 56 shields of the different parts of the empire, and motifs of the Order of the Golden Fleece, and the seven electors.

In England, masonic and heraldic emblems appeared on wine glasses, goblets, beakers and firing glasses. Those enamelled by the Beilbys during the 1760s are among the most celebrated, such as the small group of royal goblets bearing the arms of George III, with the Prince of Wales' feathers and motto on the reverse (possibly made to commemorate the birth of the prince in 1762; see p. 70).

In the U.S.A., mould-blown and brightly coloured flasks with masonic devices were produced in large numbers from c. 1820–30, at factories in New England and Ohio. Many were decorated with the American eagle on the reverse. (See also Commemorative Wares, p. 186.)

ANIMALS AND FIGURES

Representations in glass of the human figure and of animals have been manufactured widely since the 14th century BC, appearing in the form of either individual objects for display,

Armorial drinking glasses: the firing glasses, of waisted beaker form, are enamelled with the arms of the Lodge of Journeymen and Masons No. 8 (Edinburgh) on a rococo shield (*left*), and with masonic emblems (*right*); the wine glass is enamelled with an elaborate rococo shield containing a heart and crossed arrows ($7\frac{1}{8}$in). All Newcastle-on-Tyne, probably the Beilby workshop, c. 1765.

decoration or amusement; or novelty vessels assuming either the shape of an animal or figure, such as Roman head flasks, or incorporated as a component part of the vessel, such as the animal-shaped stem of some drinking glasses; or applied as individual ornaments to the exterior of a vessel (after it has been formed). All three presentations have been exploited fully and with great imagination by glass-makers throughout the world who have depicted an unlimited range of real and imaginary animals, birds, reptiles and insects, as well as portraits of contemporary celebrities and characters derived from biblical and legendary sources.

As objects in their own right. As early as the 14th century BC small glass figurines were produced in the Near East for religious and ritualistic purposes, cast initially in one-piece moulds and later in two-piece moulds for a three-dimensional effect. Some were probably worn as good-luck charms, and to ward off evil spirits. Similar pieces from China date from the 9th century AD and depict Buddhist deities and symbolic beasts such as the crouching

FOR DECORATION

Glass portraits, *left to right*
"Tragic" mask of the Greek
theatre, originally the base of a
rhyton cup, 1st century AD;
Egyptian head of Bes, c. 300
BC; and Byzantine portrait,
possibly that of Romanus II,
c. 1100 AD.

lion or *shihtzu*. Roman glass-makers created a wide range of figural subjects, including portrait busts of emperors, cast and modelled in the round like sculpture, and profiles moulded and worked in relief on small panels, such as the plaque of Bonus Eventus ("Good Success", the god of the harvest) now in the British Museum.

Figures and animals for decoration and amusement have been made throughout Europe since the 16th century. The toy-like figures which were made at Nevers and elsewhere in France during this early period achieved international recognition. These were formed from pieces of glass rod, softened and worked at the lamp and applied over supporting frames of metal wire. Similar examples were made later in England, Spain and Venice. In Barcelona, ornamental birds, reptiles and "curiosities" were produced by glass-makers in their spare time as souvenirs for tourists, or during special glass-blowing exhibitions which were held at factories across the country (see also Friggers, p. 182).

During the 19th century in England, figures and animals were manufactured, often of pressed glass. Coloured portrait busts of Queen Victoria and William Shakespeare were popular mantlepiece ornaments, produced chiefly in the Birmingham and Stourbridge areas. Long-tailed birds made at the lamp were also fashionable about 1850, arranged on glass "fountains" as centrepieces (see p. 184).

French glass-makers favoured the use of animals and figures for paperweight subjects, and later, under the influence of Art Nouveau, designers such as Almeric-V. Walter specialised in the creation of reptiles in *pâte-de-verre* (powdered glass made into a paste, coloured and formed by moulding). Perhaps the greatest exponent of all was René Lalique, whose mass-produced range of car

FOR DECORATION

mascots, radiator caps, statuettes and pendants were moulded into giant dragonflies, greyhounds, parrots and sea maidens.

Novelty vessels. Roman glass-makers produced drinking horns shaped like animals' heads, mould-blown bottles in the form of fish and grotesque heads, and helmet flasks which, when inverted, resemble the heads of warriors in helmets. Dromedary flasks of Near Eastern manufacture (6th–8th centuries AD) consist of four-legged animals supporting trellis-work vases on their backs.

Venetian glass-makers frequently used animals, such as prancing horses, on the stems of drinking glasses and shafts of candlesticks, reflecting the taste for extravagant and fantastic forms. German glass-makers produced joke drinking glasses with hollow glass straws surmounted by stags and other animals, from which the liquid was sucked (also made in Russia during the 1700s). More recently, Lalique manufactured vases in the form of cobras, scent bottles shaped like snails, etc.

Ornaments. Shellfish and dolphins were favourite motifs of Cologne glass-makers in the 4th century who applied them in circles around the exteriors of beakers. Later, the Venetians preferred lions' heads, masks and classical figural

Above A *Scherzgefäss* or puzzle goblet. The central column supports a detachable stag (used as a siphon); German, 17th century.

Right Pâte-de-verre lizard and seal coloured green and yellow, by the French glass-maker Almeric-V. Walter (1859–1942), who created numerous animal sculptures in this medium. Signed "A. WALTER, NANCY", 1920s.

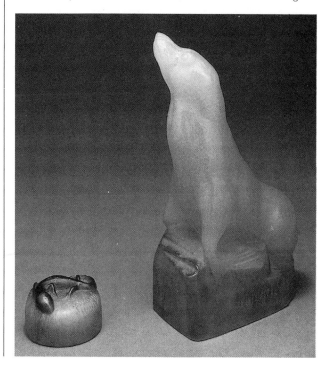

179

FOR DECORATION

scenes which were mould-blown to decorate the walls of large vessels. Nineteenth-century French and English opaline wares are frequently adorned with glass snakes, entwined around the necks of scent bottles and vases.

CENTREPIECES AND ÉPERGNES

Centrepieces of various shapes and styles were manufactured widely during the 18th and 19th centuries, primarily to serve a decorative function at the centre of the dining table. *Épergnes*, however, were designed with large bowls for holding fruit, or with numerous fittings to contain a selection of foods (see below). Both kinds of piece were made of silver, often with cut glass dishes and bowls, and also entirely of glass, particularly the most decorative and flamboyant, such as the fantastic floral and figural centrepieces created by Venetian glass-makers during the 18th century and later. Even more extravagant were the *trionfo* ("triumph") centrepieces, which consisted of miniature pieces of glass, formed at the lamp into trees,

Venetian *cristallo* centrepiece, possibly also used to display fruit, decorated with applied moulded masks and surmounted by a blue and opaque white glass finial, on bun feet. Late 17th-early 18th century.

FOR DECORATION

Right Épergne made almost entirely of glass, the branched arms supporting six cut baskets hung with pendant drops, below a central bowl. English, c.1795.

Below Victorian *épergne* of Vaseline glass, adorned with applied red trails around the rims of the trumpet-shaped vases and base. "Sugar cane" twisted rods of clear glass complete the fanciful decoration. About 1860; 21in.

plants, statues, columns etc., and arranged into formal garden landscapes. Another Venetian speciality were the moulded glass fruits and vegetables, brightly coloured and life-size, which were arranged in bowls and placed on tables as novelty or conversation pieces. In Barcelona since the late 17th century, large decorative glass birds and animals had been manufactured.

In England, glass centrepieces were produced over a long period, from about 1740 to 1910. Initially they consisted of a large bowl mounted on a tall stem to which there might be attached several branches or arms, held in place by metal sockets. Eighteenth-century styles followed those for silver, in the later years of the century reflecting neo-classical tastes in their urn-shaped stems, sometimes fitted with candle sconces for additional use as candelabra. From the mid-18th century onwards, the term *épergne* was introduced (from the French *épargner*, to save) and appeared in numerous advertisements of the period. *Épergnes* were usually designed with one or more of the following: bread, cake and bonbon baskets, fruit and sweetmeat dishes, condiment containers and, later, vases for flowers – each

FOR DECORATION

receptacle attached to or hung from branch-like arms which projected from the central stand. *Épergnes* were originally intended as space-saving devices, and to prevent the diners from having to pass dishes around the table. During the 19th century, however, the *épergne* became more massive and elaborate. By c.1850, it was commonly transformed into a flower stand 1–2 feet high, consisting of several trumpet- or basket-shaped vases arranged around a larger central vase, mounted on a saucer-type base or on mirror glass (known as a *plateau*). A number were equipped with branches as before, but now decorated extravagantly with large leaves of coloured glass, trailed and pincered threads, frilled borders and other applied motifs – reflecting Victorian tastes for ostentatious display. Large numbers were manufactured at factories in London and Stourbridge, and exported until c.1890 to North America (where only a few *épergnes* were produced, for example at the Boston and Sandwich Glass Company, modelled on English prototypes).

FRIGGERS

This general term describes a wide range of decorative but impractical objects, some created by glass-makers in their spare time for amusement, others more commercially for sale at country fairs etc., usually from left-over and re-melted waste glass remaining in the factory pots after the day's work – hence, the term "end-of-day wares".

Friggers were produced in Spain and elsewhere in Europe from the 16th century onwards. Miniature top hats, buckets, large tobacco pipes, birds, lizards and farm animals were blown in both clear and coloured glass, sometimes decorated with applied pincered threads and other pieces of brightly coloured glass to form eyes, beaks and tails. Many were probably sold as souvenirs, or used to decorate the interiors of workmens' cottages.

Among the friggers made in large numbers in the late 18th and 19th centuries, particularly in England and America (where they were known as whimseys), are glass bells coloured in clear and opaque shades, sometimes with mottled decoration and surmounted by hand-shaped finials. Other friggers catered to superstition: walking sticks and canes 3 to 6 feet long, said to have been hung to attract germs and diseases, and wiped down daily; witch-balls (3–7 inches diameter), also hung or placed on mantlepieces to ward off evil spirits; and hollow rolling pins (about 1 foot long) of various colours and frequently with painted inscriptions, traditionally given by sailors to their wives before departing to sea. Those pins with a stoppered end may also have been used for smuggling spirits, as well as (filled with cold water) simply for pastry-making. The

Right Glass pipe, a popular form of frigger, decorated in the Nailsea filigree style with threads of opaque white and red within the clear metal. English, early 19th century; 30in.

Below Rolling pin friggers: *top* of blue glass, enamelled and inscribed "Remember Me"; *bottom* decorated in the Nailsea style, with swirling threads of opaque white; English, early 19th century; 13in.

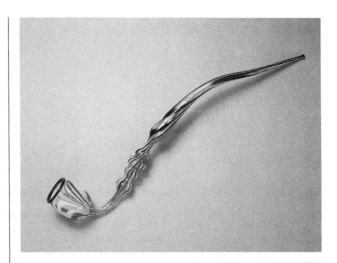

majority were free-blown and decorated with combed coloured loops, speckles or filigree threads in the "Nailsea" style (see p. 215). Other objects such as bird fountains (exotic long-tailed birds placed on glass fountains), model ships, miniature lighthouses and cottages are often described today as friggers, but it is more likely that these were the commercial products of small workshops intended for display under glass domes in Victorian parlours. They were usually made at the lamp, using glass fibres to represent the sea water and individual strands for the long tails of birds.

Elaborate "bird fountain" under a clear glass dome, the opaque white birds adorned with threads of pink, blue and green, and glass fibres for the tails and frothy base. English, c. 1850; 17in.

DOMES

Glass domes were made in France from the 18th century to encase glass figurines (such as those made at Nevers), and elsewhere in Europe to protect clocks from dust and damp. Many large domes or "shades" were made in 19th-century England to cover and protect parlour displays of wax fruits, artificial flowers, stuffed birds and animals, glass ships and "bird fountains". Victorian domes were made by the "broad" process (also used for windows) by blowing and working a bubble of glass into a rounded cylindrical shape, then cutting one end (leaving the other end dome-shaped) and re-heating for a smooth finish.

MANTELPIECE DECORATION

Among the many objects for mantelpiece display manufactured in the 19th century are vase lustres, usually in pairs

FOR DECORATION

and consisting of goblet-shaped vessels with serrated rims from which were hung cut glass pendant drops, produced in Bohemia and imitated in England with gilded and painted floral designs and portraits; moulded portrait busts of celebrities, popular in England c. 1850; witch-balls (see Friggers, p. 182) mounted on tall vases, and Devil's Fire ornaments made to resemble pine trees (about 11 inches high) and decorated with splashes or "flames" of coloured glass – both made in the U.S.A.

NEFS
These decorative sailing ships (10–14 inches high) were introduced during the late mediaeval period, when they were placed ceremoniously before the host at the table. Most were metal, but several of glass were designed at Murano from c. 1521 by Ermonia Vivarini, who was granted

Above Pair of storm shades painted with floral bouquets and mounted on tall stands designed for a mantelpiece. English; c. 1830.

Right Nef ewer (*navicello*) of *cristallo* glass, adorned with applied blue masks and trails, attributed to Arminia (Ermonia) Vivarini, c. 1550; 11$\frac{1}{3}$in high.

FOR DECORATION

the exclusive right for their production. Glass nefs *à la façon de Venise* were probably also manufactured by the Colinet family of Beauwelz in Belgium, such as the one commissioned for Emperor Charles V in 1549 (which survives only in sketch-form). Others were made in the Low Countries and England during the 17th and early 18th centuries.

Several ewers were designed as nefs – the spout, which projected from the blown bowl (or hull) forms the prow and an intricate network of glass threads (made at the lamp) provides the rigging. The top or masthead was sometimes surmounted with a dolphin or other decorative finial, and the sides were adorned with applied strawberry prunts and moulded lions' masks. Venetian examples (*navicelli*) were of colourless *cristallo* glass, characteristically edged in bright blue and other shades, and mounted on a knopped and stemmed foot. This style was copied widely.

COMMEMORATIVE WARES

Among the oldest glass surviving are three small core-formed vessels bearing the cartouche of the Egyptian ruler Tuthmosis III (c. 1479–1425 BC) and hieroglyphic inscriptions. During the 13th and 14th centuries AD, dedications to the sultans of Islam were enamelled commonly on hanging mosque lamps. In Europe, tributes to kings and queens appeared, chiefly on goblets and drinking glasses, from the late 16th century onwards, including portraits and inscriptions to commemorate births, marriages, accessions and jubilees.

Wine glass engraved on the double-ogee bowl with a wreath of flowers including a Jacobite rose, set on an air-twist stem. English, c. 1750.

Battles, peace treaties, political campaigns and statesmen have been portrayed on European glass since the 17th century. In England, Jacobite emblems were engraved on 18th-century drinking glasses in support of the exiled James II (deposed in 1698) and the Stuart line of succession. Portraits, such as that of Bonnie Prince Charlie (the "Young Pretender"), symbols (the rose with buds, the thistle) and mottoes (e.g. "Audentior Ibo" meaning "I shall go more boldly") were all used to commemorate the 1715 and 1745 Jacobite rebellions long after the cause was lost. In the U.S.A., mould-blown historical flasks were produced in enormous numbers c. 1800–80, decorated with portraits of presidents, celebrities, naval vessels and nationalistic symbols – portraying over 400 themes in all.

Roman glass-makers decorated vessels with chariot races, prize fights and gladiatorial scenes, frequently combined with laurels, inscriptions and the names of contestants – for commemorative purposes and possibly intended as prizes. During the 17th century, Bohemian and German craftsmen enamelled *Humpen* and other wares with elaborate hunting scenes depicting stags, bears and rabbits pursued by hunters on horseback. Dutch and

FOR DECORATION

English engravers employed coaching scenes, angling subjects, card games, etc. on goblets and other drinking glasses, often commissioned by clubs and companies for presentation purposes.

VASES

Manufactured since Roman times, glass vases for decorative display and for holding flowers have appeared in an enormous range of shapes, sizes and styles. Undoubtedly one of the finest surviving pieces is the "Portland Vase" (1st century BC or 1st century AD) of Greek amphora shape, the dark blue body overlaid in opaque white and cut in cameo relief on all sides. Thought to depict the marriage of Peleus and Thetis, the vase displays the immense technical mastery and artistic refinement of Roman glass-making, which was to have a considerable impact in the 19th century, resulting in the commercial production of cameo glass (see below).

When fine glass-making was resumed in Europe by the 15th century, vases featured prominently amongst the artistic and luxury wares created for the courts and the wealthy. As ornamental vessels, they encouraged glass-makers to experiment freely with new shapes and techniques which were not, of necessity, bound to a specific function. In Venice, vases were often of ice glass or filigree glass with applied coloured threads around rims and handles and moulded lions' masks on the body, or with classical figural scenes in relief. Novelty vases were also produced, some displaying imitation glass flowers and leaves which projected from the top of the vessel, others with transparent walls enclosing small porcelain *putti* or glass bouquets attached to the base. In England, opaque white vases of inverted baluster shape were produced in the

1750s and 1760s, in imitation of contemporary Chinese porcelain, painted in *famille rose* colours with *chinoiserie* figure decoration of courtly ladies, scholars, hunters, exotic birds and flowers. In China from 1750, three main styles of decorative vase evolved: those resembling porcelain (as above); mould-blown in translucent colours with relief panels enclosing symbolic motifs; and overlaid in bright opaque shades and cut cameo-fashion with stylised flowers and geometric patterns.

Vases achieved their greatest popularity in the second half of the 19th century, when they were manufactured throughout Europe and in the U.S.A. English firms in the Stourbridge and Birmingham areas created opaline vases decorated with classical scenes (e.g. by Richardson), cameo vases overlaid in delicate shades and cut meticulously with naturalistic flowers (e.g. by Thomas Webb), and vases adorned with applied glass fruits and flowers. In France, *millefiori* vases were made by Clichy, and in Bohemia the popular flashed style was adopted, with cut "windows" and enamelled and gilded flowers. In the 1880s American vases reflected current tastes for the new colour effects of art glass – e.g. Peachblow, Satin, and Amberina.

Art Nouveau vases were rendered frequently in exotic forms which followed the sinuous asymmetrical lines of the style, their surfaces displaying a range of effects, from the brilliant iridescence of Tiffany and Loetz, to the serene landscapes of Gallé and Daum. Later (c.1920–30), Lalique designed and mass-produced over 200 styles of vase in clear, opalescent and coloured glass. Outstanding examples include vases with figural scenes in high relief (probably made in the power press), others with massive side-handles – polished and pierced with geometric designs, and those adorned with giant cobras, parrots, cockerels and fish. Several were reproduced by Cristallerie Lalique after World War II.

PERSONAL USE

SCENT BOTTLES

These small bottles, usually with a ground glass stopper or a metal top, were intended for perfumes, scented oils and essences. Examples have been excavated from ancient Egyptian tombs (from c. 1400 BC): it was customary for aromatic preparations to be used during religious and funerary ceremonies, and for embalming. The small core-formed bottles were brightly coloured in opaque shades to imitate semi-precious stones, and decorated with threads of contrasting colours in zig-zag and wavy patterns. By the 7th and 6th centuries BC, Egyptian scent bottles followed the forms of Greek ceramic prototypes, and shapes such as the tubular *alabastron* and the globular *aryballos* (probably used for bath oils and suspended from the wrist by a cord) were adopted widely in the Mediterranean area. Perfumes were often worn by the nobility, and large numbers of bottles survive from the 6th–1st centuries BC and were depicted in contemporary tomb paintings.

With the discovery of glass-blowing, Roman craftsmen

Opaline glass scent bottle of apple green colour, with pierced gilt-metal sides and top. French, c. 1840.

extended the range of scent bottles to contain aromatic herbs and oils – used for ritualistic burials and as aphrodisiacs. Bottles were mould-blown into novelty shapes (e.g. fish and human heads), decorated over the surface in relief with miniature urns, or blown simply following Greek forms. The transparent colours were restricted chiefly to browns, purples and greens, although bottles of mosaic glass, and those in imitation of natural stones, were created for an elite market. After the collapse of the Roman empire coloured scent bottles (frequently cut and engraved with geometric motifs) were manufactured in the Near East for local and export markets.

By the 15th century, Venetian glass-makers were probably producing scent bottles for the courts and the wealthy. Few examples, however, can be dated before the 16th century, when scent bottles were made of colourless *cristallo* glass rendered into simple but elegant forms and adorned with threads of bright blue trailed around the handles, rims and feet. During the 17th century, styles became increasingly flamboyant and coloured glass finials, winged handles and elaborately fashioned stems featured commonly, to be imitated in Spain and the Netherlands in keeping with popular demands for perfume and Venetian-style glass.

In France, scent was manufactured as early as the 12th century. Later, during the reigns of Louis XIV and Louis XV, perfume became highly fashionable and the court was supplied daily with a different fragrance for spraying clothes, accessories and ornamental objects. The expensive perfumes were housed in individual bottles of richly coloured glass mounted in gold and silver, such as those moulded in relief with hearts and the heraldic fleur-de-lis attributed to the Italian glass-maker Bernard Perrot (who worked at Orléans from 1662).

The finest scent bottles were undoubtedly produced during the 18th century, when famous perfumiers such as Houbigant became established, and when glass shapes and styles conformed to an overall elegance and refinement which complemented their costly contents. *Milchglas* bottles of German and Bohemian manufacture were finely enamelled with floral bouquets and pastoral scenes in delicate shades. Other bottles from these countries were decorated by engraving on clear glass. In England, coloured scent bottles in blue, green and purple were enamelled with naturalistic flowers, exotic birds and *chinoiserie* designs, diamond-faceted and surmounted by gold repoussé tops (the latter designed by jewellers and goldsmiths). Some were made in pairs with shagreen protective cases for travelling. Bottles of opaque white glass made to resemble fine porcelain were produced in the Bristol, Birmingham

PERSONAL USE

and south Staffordshire areas, again enamelled by the independent decorators commissioned to adorn both glass and ceramic objects. Such bottles have been attributed tentatively to the workshops of James Giles and Michael Edkins, but it is more likely that a large number of freelance decorators were employed.

During the 19th century, fine scent bottles continued to be made in France (*millefiori* and opaline), England (cameo) and Bohemia (flashed). More recently, glass-makers have been commissioned by perfume manu-facturers to create exclusive ranges of bottles: Gallé designed for Guerlain, and Lalique for Coty, Nina Ricci, and Worth.

JEWELLERY

Glass has been employed for jewellery for over 3,500 years – shaped into beads, pendants and bangles, set in gold and silver to imitate precious and semi-precious stones, and inlaid piece by piece to create pictorial compositions or mosaics. The range of presentations is vast, frequently demonstrating the combined skills of the glass-maker and jeweller, and the development of glass technology as it was adapted to meet fashionable tastes.

Above Pair of blue tinted scent bottles gilded with *genre* scenes and flowers on the stoppers. By the Spanish factory of La Granja de San Ildefonso, c. 1780.

Right Fine opaque white glass scent bottle of shouldered form, faceted with diamonds over the surface and decorated in gold and coloured enamels depicting exotic birds, insects, fruits and flowering branches. Surmounted by a gold spiral repoussé top. London or south Staffordshire, c. 1760.

PERSONAL USE

Beads

Pierced and strung into necklaces, worn as pendants and earrings, important and easily transported articles of trade, beads have been manufactured in the Near East since ancient times. Early examples (c. 1500 BC) were usually of spherical or cylindrical form and made from small pieces of molten glass rod, re-heated, pierced, shaped and stamped whilst soft to incorporate threads and dots of glass for decoration, and ground for a smooth finish. Many were coloured opaque blue, to imitate the highly prized lapis lazuli, adorned with spots and stripes of yellow and opaque white. "Eye" beads appeared by c. 1000 BC, usually coloured opaque bluish-black with white or yellow eye motifs applied and pressed into the soft glass. From the 6th century BC decoration became increasingly flamboyant and the surfaces of beads were covered with brightly coloured threads in spiral, zig-zag and wavy patterns, or beads were sometimes shaped into grotesque human

Roman multi-coloured glass beads, some featuring iridescence on the surface. 2nd century AD; average diameter ½in.

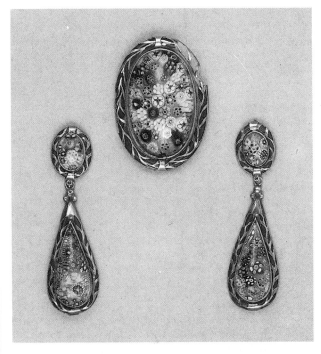

Brooch and drop earrings composed of multi-coloured *millefiori* canes, edged with dark blue glass in a gold framework. Probably Bohemian, 19th century.

heads. Styles altered little during the Roman period, and beads of Near Eastern manufacture were exported throughout Europe, where they catered to regional superstitions and customs, and possibly to the Far East as suggested by large numbers excavated in Japanese tombs. In Britain, they were thought to possess magical properties; in the Rhineland they were presented to heroic soldiers; and in Celtic religious orders, they were worn by Druid priests to denote rank and status. The Romans also manufactured beads of *millefiori* and mosaic glass, distinguished by their complex designs and multi-coloured surfaces. Large numbers of beads were made in Venice from the 12th century onwards, created by specialist craftsmen known as the *margaritai* (makers of small beads), and the *perlai* (of large hollow ones). Later, fine quality beads were produced in central Europe (e.g. enamelled or engraved) in keeping with contemporary tastes, and more recently machine-made examples have been used for costume jewellery. During the Art Deco period, beads were frequently moulded into flat, geometric shapes.

Inlays
Pieces of coloured glass, set and mounted – usually on metal – for simple adornment and patterning, have often

been used as a substitute for semi-precious stones. Egyptian gold pendants and bracelets, inlaid with pieces of opaque blue glass, have survived from c. 1600 BC. Later in Egypt (c. 600–100 BC), pieces of glass were set in cloisons, as in enamel work, each small section delineated and held in place by metal wires. Glass inlays were also used to decorate Anglo-Saxon ornaments, including silver-gilt belt buckles, shoulder clasps and brooches. Such items have been excavated in graves from Ireland to Scandinavia, inset with pieces of red, blue and white *millefiori* glass, and decorated with zoomorphic designs. *Millefiori* continues to be used for jewellery to this day.

Fine 18th- and early 19th-century French and English paste jewellery, displaying a wide range of colours including turquoise, pink, purple and amber.

Mosaics

In mosaic, small pieces of opaque coloured glass (*tesserae*) are arranged into geometric patterns or pictorial compositions and held together with a cement mixed from crushed stone, sand and water. Glass and other materials were employed for mosaic jewellery in Roman times, a technique revived in Italy during the Renaissance period, when two important workshops were established about 1580 in Florence and Rome. The latter specialised in glass pictorial mosaics, depicting figural subjects and pastoral scenes derived from well-known paintings and frescoes, and sold to tourists as souvenirs. Brooches, earrings and necklaces were composed of small mosaic plaques arranged and linked together, and the glass *tesserae* imitated successfully the subtleties of tone and shading conveyed by the painter's brush.

Methods of manufacture altered little until c. 1750, when the technique of micromosaics was introduced at the Vatican workshop. By this method, coloured glass rods were pulled and elongated into thin strips, called *smalti filati*, from which could be obtained innumerable hues for every colour. The strips were then cut into minute pieces, each possessing its own subtle tint. Micromosaics improved greatly the process of accurate colour reproduction, and the finest work, such as that executed by Giacomo Raffaelli c. 1775, achieved considerable recognition. The technique continued to be employed during the 19th century for matching jewellery sets, notably by Antonio Aguatti and Michelangelo Barberi c. 1820–60.

Paste

Small pieces of glass, cut, faceted and set to imitate diamonds, rubies and other gemstones, were manufactured during the 18th and early 19th centuries in England, France and Spain. The use of lead glass was found to be most suitable for the production of paste – having a high refractive index, weight and brilliance, which could be used

PERSONAL USE

to imitate successfully the then popular and expensive rose-cut diamond. The finest examples of paste jewellery were made by George Frederic Strass (1702–73) who employed lead glass at his Paris workshop from c. 1730 to create an exquisite range of tiaras, necklaces, bow-brooches and buckles – all meticulously finished, copying faithfully the closed settings of fashionable diamond prototypes. Indeed, the name Strass is today synonymous with fine paste. The soft glass could be cut easily and more imaginatively than diamonds, encouraging further experimentation in the faceting by virtue of its low cost and wide availability. Coloured and opal pastes were also produced, enclosed and backed with tinted foil to enhance the hue, and to prevent corrosion. By the mid-19th century, however, the quality of paste had declined due to changing fashions and falling demand. The technique was revived during the Art Deco period (e.g. by Cartier) when the vogue for diamonds returned.

Chinese glass snuff bottles. *Left to right* Four cameo bottles; round "imperial yellow" bottle; painted-inside bottle dated 1897; opaque white bottle of double-gourd form with enamelled birds and foliage; pink translucent bottle in imitation of quartz; and bottle in the form of a peach. All from 1750–1900; average height 3in.

SNUFF BOTTLES

Snuff bottles were produced in China from about 1700, initially for the Manchu court at Peking, but after c. 1780 for popular use, as snuff-taking in China became a national pastime. Over a period of two centuries an imaginative range of styles evolved, although the majority conformed to the standard shape of a short-necked, flat-sided jar about 2 inches high with a glass or stone dome-shaped top and cork stopper, to which was attached a small spoon for removing the snuff. By the early 20th century, the quality of bottles had declined, although recently the craft has been revived and fine examples have been exported widely. Pieces are difficult to date, but period attributions can be made on the basis of style and technique.

Monochrome bottles were made in rich opaque shades, or with mottled tonal effects such as "snowflake" glass with its translucent and granular surface to simulate white jadeite; manufactured from c. 1700.

Enamelled bottles – the painting often executed on opaque white or pastel-coloured glass in imitation of porcelain, with delicate floral patterns, landscapes and figural subjects – were made from c. 1725 onwards (some with carved reign marks on the base, filled in with coloured enamel).

Cameo bottles were frequently composed of white glass overlaid in red and green – but sometimes incorporating up to five different shades – and cut in relief with flowers. leafy sprays and symbolic motifs to create a rich sculptured effect, in imitation of coloured hardstones; made from c. 1740. Bottles were also decorated with applied blobs of glass, coloured and decorated to imitate cameo.

Bottles painted inside were created by painting on the interior walls using a fine brush or pen through the narrow top of the bottle. The design was executed in reverse, to be viewed from the outside – an arduous and painstaking process, executed by Peking watercolourists from c. 1800 in muted shades, and elsewhere in China during the 1900s in vivid colours. Recent examples tend to be of poor quality, although a few reflect an outstanding technical mastery. A bottle made in 1972 by Li Kechang of the Shantung School was painted inside with 292 individual figures, 15 oxen and 6 horses! In early examples, the interior surfaces are rough and pitted, but later acid was employed to achieve a smooth finish, and to prevent the paint from flaking. Many examples are signed.

In Europe, containers for snuff were rarely of glass, but in the U.S.A., bottles were manufactured in the New Jersey area c. 1880–1900, at the Williamstown Glass Factory, and at the Fairton Glass Works where square olive-green and amber bottles were produced.

PERSONAL USE

Snuff bottle of olive green glass, pattern-moulded and free-blown, of a type associated with the Pitkin Glass works of Connecticut (hence, sometimes referred to as a "Pitkin flask", although the style was adopted elsewhere, throughout the Mid-West and New England). Early 19th century.

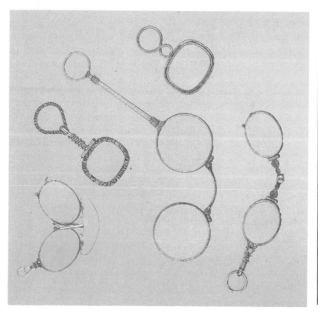

Popular 19th-century vision aids, showing two lorgnettes, a ladies' spy glass, quizzing glass, and pince-nez. All mounted in gold or pinchbeck.

EYE GLASSES AND SCIENTIFIC INSTRUMENTS

Spectacles of simple construction were probably first made in Italy during the late 13th century and, having convex lenses, were exclusively for the long-sighted. With the development of the printing press in the 15th century, the demand for spectacles increased greatly amongst the literate classes of Europe, shortly followed by the application of the concave lens to aid the short-sighted. The quality of lenses, however, improved only gradually, marred as it was by defects in the clarity of the glass and by the presence of air bubbles. Lenses of clear and green-tinted "forest" glass were made during the 16th century by spectacle-makers in Germany and the Low Countries, and at Sir Robert Mansell's factories in England (after c. 1630) using sheets of higher quality glass. By the late 18th century, English lenses, often housed in ornate frames of gold, silver and horn, were being produced to meet a growing European demand. Thereafter, a large number of fashionable vision aids were introduced, including: monocles, single lenses sometimes mounted on metal circular frames; lorgnettes, folding pairs of lenses on decorative frames and handles, worn by ladies on a chain around the neck (and later clipped like a brooch c. 1925); *pince-nez*, two lenses on a metal frame that clip to the nose; opera-glasses, introduced c. 1750 in the form of a telescope, but later designed with twin lenses and housed in ornate cases.

The extensive progress of science during the 17th century depended ultimately on precise observation achieved by the use of new and accurate scientific instruments, among them the telescope, microscope and barometer (all made partly of glass). The development of the telescope and compound microscope related directly to the production of fine quality glass lenses, as probably first made by spectacle-makers in northern Europe c. 1600 and afterwards improved and refined by Galileo for astronomical use. By c. 1650, telescopes were being produced in France, England (at Mansell's factories) and in the Low Countries. Telescopes were employed widely – for military and naval purposes, and for astronomical study – but the development of the microscope was relatively slow, as the instrument was of limited practical use and regarded by scientists as a curious toy until the second half of the 17th century. During this period, when scientific pursuits became fashionable amongst wealthy patrons in England and Italy, numerous other inventions and improvements occurred which depended, to a large extent, on glass manufacture. Perhaps most important, at least in numbers used, were the glass test-tubes, phials, flasks and other accessories employed in scientific experiments.

WALLS AND WINDOWS

LOOKING GLASSES

For centuries mirrors have served a functional and a decorative purpose, being employed at the dressing table for personal use, and displayed in interiors to give the illusion of space and to reflect light. Polished bronze and other metal mirrors have survived of ancient Greek and Chinese manufacture; they were reproduced by Roman craftsmen and continued to be made throughout the Middle Ages, when "speculum" (an alloy of copper and tin) and occasionally expensive rock crystal were employed, being considered superior to any metal-backed glass then obtainable, less fragile and able to sustain a high polish.

Glass mirrors were not made commonly before the mid-16th century, although a few convex looking glasses (reflecting a reduced image) had been produced since the early 1400s in Nuremberg and south Germany, as depicted in Van Eyck's portrait of Giovanni Arnolfini and Giovanna Cenami, 1434 (in the National Gallery, London). In Venice, glass mirrors were made by the early 1500s, and a mirror-makers' guild was founded in 1564.

For the next 150 years, Venetian looking glasses were exported to palaces and wealthy residences throughout Europe, superseding their metal prototypes and highly prized. The method used in their production, called the Lorraine, or "broad" process, was complicated and the size and quality of the resultant glass depended much upon the skills of the craftsman. A large bubble was blown and elongated into a cylindrical shape. The hemispherical ends were sheared off, and a slit made lengthwise, enabling the cylinder to be rolled open as a sheet. After re-heating and flattening, the glass was annealed, polished and "silvered" using an amalgam of mercury and tin-foil. Sheet glass made by this process was of a relatively small size (maximum height about 4 feet) so that large wall mirrors invariably consisted of several plates arranged together. Venetian mirror techniques soon spread to France, Germany, the Low Countries and England, but examples continued to be exported from Venice in large numbers. During the early 17th century in England, when imports were banned, looking glasses were made by Sir Robert Mansell, and after his death by the 2nd Duke of Buckingham, who established a sheet glass and mirror factory at Vauxhall, south London, in c. 1663.

Towards the end of the 17th century, a new and successful process of casting sheets of glass (adapted from the Roman technique of "casting": see Early Window Glass, below) was introduced (1687) in France by Bernard Perrot by which could be produced larger "plates" of an even thickness and superior quality. This was achieved by pouring molten glass onto an iron table with raised edges,

Venetian mirror with tortoiseshell sides and borders of coloured and engraved glass, the corners adorned with bouquets of applied flowers. About 1860; 14in high.

Overleaf The Banker and his Wife, by the Flemish artist Quinten Massys (or Metsys, c.1465–1530), dated 1514. The small convex mirror on the table reflects a contrasting scene, that of a man reading by a window with a distant view of a church – recalling the virtues of a contemplative life, in a world of false values.

rolling it with a metal bar for smoothness, then removing it carefully for annealing, extensive polishing and silvering. Pieces were frequently bevelled (i.e. softly angled on the outer edges) c.1690–1710, and thereafter according to period styles. The casting process had been developed further by Louis-Lucas de Nehou of Normandy, and later at the Saint Gobain factory he founded in 1695 in Picardy. The large sheets were imported (and smuggled) into England at great expense until 1773, when their manufacture was introduced at the British Cast Plate Glass Co. at Ravenhead near St. Helens, Lancashire (now part of Pilkington's, inventors of the modern float glass method of producing plate glass). In Spain, large cast sheets of glass (some 13 feet high) were produced at the factory of La Granja de San Ildefonso during the second half of the 18th century for royal residences and wealthy patrons.

Various improvements in mirror glass manufacture occurred during the 19th century. The old "broad" method was made more productive by the Birmingham manufacturer Robert Lucas Chance c.1830 by creating larger glass cylinders. The process of silvering was also refined by the German chemist Justus von Liebig in 1835, by

depositing a thin layer of pure silver on the surface of the glass, the back of which was then coated with red lead or paint for greater durability.

EARLY WINDOW GLASS

Glazed windows came into use by the 1st century AD, particularly in northern regions of the Roman empire. Two methods of manufacture were employed: casting the molten glass, by pouring it into a shallow mould and smoothing it, or blowing the glass in the "broad" process (see Looking Glasses), as used extensively during later periods of window- and mirror-glass manufacture.

During the Middle Ages, window glass was made for luxury markets in the forest glass-houses of France (especially the prestigious centres in Normandy and Lorraine), the Low Countries, parts of Germany and elsewhere in Europe. The leaded windows were made in two ways. The first, the old "broad" method, was retained and improved in the late 14th century in Lorraine by increasing the size of the cylinders to obtain large and even sheets. From these, numerous panes were cut, arranged geometrically (often into lozenge patterns) and held in place by lead strips. The wood-framed windows were then ready to be installed, and so highly valued were they that if the house was sold, the windows moved with the owner.

The second technique, known as the "crown" process, was also executed on the blow-pipe, by manipulating the glass into a flattened globe to which was attached another metal rod, or pontil. The blow-pipe was then cracked off, and the globe re-heated and whirled rapidly to form a flat disc. When the pontil was removed, a thick swirl of glass remained in the centre, known as a bull's eye. The large disc or "crown" was cut into small panes, which were arranged in parallel rows to form the surface of the window. The intervening gaps between the roundels were filled in with triangular pieces of cut glass. "Crown" glass was highly favoured in Normandy and elsewhere in Europe, and although its subsequent cutting into panes was a somewhat arduous task (made more complicated by the bull's eye) it also yielded a smooth and highly polished surface.

The Norman and Lorrainer families were acclaimed throughout Europe as the finest specialists of window glass and their windows were exported widely. In England, the mediaeval forest glass-houses of the Weald also made window glass, but undoubtedly much of superior quality was imported from abroad. By c. 1580–90, however, window glass production improved substantially in England. Jean Carré, with the aid of craftsmen from Normandy and Lorraine, established two furnaces in the Weald for its manufacture, and other specialist factories

The manufacture of "crown" glass, showing the various stages of blowing and rapid whirling. From *The Saturday Magazine*, London, 5th October, 1833.

were founded. As a result, the expensive imports soon gave way to cheaper, home-produced window glass, which now could be afforded by those of moderate means. In addition, windows were used in carriages, and also in ships.

Few complete domestic windows have survived from this period, although examples were sometimes depicted in contemporary paintings, such as those by the 17th-century Dutch artist Vermeer. In his interior scenes, the windows are hinged to their wooden frames to open inwards, with shutters on the exterior for protection. Earlier, the glass was confined to the top portion of the window, with wooden shutters below. Individual panes were sometimes enamelled or engraved with heraldic motifs and figural scenes for decoration.

The discovery of casting large sheets of glass (see Looking Glasses) resulted in the appearance of expansive windows, usually reserved for courtly residences (as at Versailles in the 1680s), which rose from the floor to the cornice. The use of lead for tall windows was replaced to a large extent by wood during the late 17th century, wood being lighter and inexpensive. In England, wood was employed most significantly in the design of sash windows, introduced at Windsor Castle in 1686. Thereafter, wood-framed windows are increasingly common in Europe (and in North America after c. 1740).

STAINED GLASS
Stained glass windows were erected in large numbers from the 12th century onwards in the large and imposing late Romanesque and early Gothic cathedrals and abbeys of northwest Europe (in Greece, Italy and Byzantium, glass mosaics were preferred for church decoration). The coloured glass was supplied by factories throughout the region, particularly those which specialised in the making of fine window glass, as in Lorraine and Normandy. It is likely that much of the glass was exported freely from country to country, exclusively to meet the church's demand for new windows. After the glass had been made and delivered to its destination, the window was created and constructed by specialist designers and glaziers. The first step was to select and sketch the subject, which in mediaeval times was invariably biblical. The glass sheets were then cut roughly with a hot iron, according to the required colour scheme and pattern, and trimmed into smaller shapes (usually roundels, squares or lozenges) by chipping the edges with a grozing iron (thus leaving a rough, serrated edge – found on most stained glass until the early 18th century, when diamond cutting was employed for a smooth finish). The brilliantly coloured pieces of glass (reds and blues were characteristic of the Gothic period) were assembled, leaded

Large stained glass window from the west end of Chartres cathedral, late 12th century. The brilliant colours and narrative content, depicting the life of the young Jesus, characterise the stained glass productions of the Gothic period.

together, and supported by iron cross-bars to form the intricate iconographic designs of the window. Famous examples of this early style can be found at the cathedrals of Augsburg (thought to house the oldest surviving stained glass, c. 1065), Poitiers, Chartres and Canterbury. Much mediaeval glass is of an irregular thickness and characterised by impurities and air bubbles, which cause the light to be refracted, and coloured throughout with metallic oxides. During the 14th century, yellow "staining" (derived from a silver compound) was painted and subsequently fired onto the surface of the glass, ranging in tone from a pale lemon to deep orange (according to the potency of the solution, and kiln conditions). By the 16th century, the technique of painting *en grisaille* using a greyish-coloured pigment (derived from iron oxide and fired) was combined with the yellow stain for costumes and hair, and superseded the use of richly coloured fragments of glass. This type of work was practised extensively in northern Europe by individual painters who derived their subjects from contemporary prints and engravings. The thematic range was also extended to include mythological and genre scenes, sometimes depicting the arms of the wealthy patron who commissioned the window. Much of the painting was executed on small roundels of clear colourless glass (average diameter 9 inches), and varied considerably in quality. Red enamel was added later to the stained and dark-outlined format, and by the 17th century the palette was enlarged further to include a variety of rich enamel shades. The former roundel now became more ovoid in shape (average size $9\frac{1}{2}$ by $7\frac{1}{2}$ inches) although still composed of colourless glass so as not to detract from the painted colour scheme.

During the late 17th and the 18th centuries, the art of glass staining declined except in the Netherlands, where examples continued to be made, probably for palaces and wealthy homes, decorated with floral bouquets and genre scenes. There was a revival of the art in the second half of the 19th and early 20th centuries – not only as a result of the refurbishing of old churches and the erecting of new ones, but also in keeping with contemporary tastes for hand craftsmanship and the return to mediaevalist ideals. In England, Sir Edward Burne-Jones and William Morris designed many windows, among them a set for Winchester cathedral, and in the U.S.A., John La Farge, and later Tiffany and the Pittsburgh firm of L. Grosse, became famous for their art glass windows, many of which were made for the homes of the wealthy as well as for churches.

Left Leaded stained glass window in the Pre-Raphaelite style, inscribed with the words "Knowledge like Fruit should not be used ... until fully Matured". Scottish school, c. 1900.

Right Stained glass roundel with the badge and cypher of Edward VI as Prince of Wales. A similar piece from Cowick Priory in Devon is in the Victoria and Albert Museum, London – on both, "Ich Dien" appears as "Hic Dein". The border decoration is a naive interpretation of Italian Renaissance themes, popular in England during the 16th century. English, first half of the 16th century; $14\frac{1}{2}$in diameter.

GLASS PICTURES
Plaques and panels
Colourful mosaic wall panels were made at Alexandria from the 1st century BC of small glass *tesserae* arranged in pictorial compositions and embedded in cement. Such work (*opus sectile*) was reserved for the finest Roman villas. Smaller mosaic plaques were also produced, frequently decorated with portraits and floral designs and made from sections of glass rods which were fused in the kiln. Others were moulded in high relief such as the 1st-century "Bonus Eventus" plaque (see p. 178), perhaps originally displayed on a piece of furniture or on the base of a candelabrum.

During the 17th and 18th centuries, small glass plaques enamelled and cold-painted in Venice depicted picturesque city views derived from contemporary paintings and prints. In Bohemia, Germany and Spain, clear glass plaques were sometimes engraved with commemorative scenes, such as that by Félix Ramos (late 18th century) featuring the façade of the Royal Palace of San Ildefonso (Museo Arqueológico

WALLS AND WINDOWS

Nacional, Madrid). More recently, *Hochschnitt* plaques (i.e. engraved in high relief) have been made by the German glass-maker Wilhelm von Eiff (1890–1943) depicting figural subjects in a contemporary manner, and also by René Lalique, who designed ornamental panels (some 6 feet high) for interior and architectural schemes.

Oil and watercolour pictures
Painting on the surface of glass (in a manner akin to that executed on canvas or board) was practised extensively by amateur artists in central Europe from the 17th century onwards.

Mirror paintings
These involved painting in oils on the reverse side of mirror glass (sometimes called back painting), first by tracing the desired pattern onto the back of the glass, then scraping off the metal-foil to reveal on the front the design to be painted. The technique was practised in England from the late 17th century, and from the 1760s in China (especially Canton) for the European market, using imported English mirror glass and contemporary prints as sources for subjects.

Transfer-engraved pictures
This complicated process was carried out in several stages: the glass, usually a thin sheet, was coated with turpentine and dried; a paper print (often a mezzotint) was soaked in water, partly dried, and placed face-down on the glass, then the back sponged, covered with water and pressed to remove air bubbles; finally the paper was carefully removed, leaving behind a dark ink outline on the glass, which was finally painted with coloured oils. Transfer-engraved pictures, popular in England c. 1670–1880, are rarely signed.

Verre églomisé
Glass ware with gold or silver leaf applied to the surface (usually the reverse side), then engraved and sometimes coloured, using oil paints and lacquers. For protection, the worked surface was then covered with another sheet of glass, metal-foil or varnish. Although the technique was known during the Roman period, its development as an artistic medium was not fully exploited until the late 18th century in France and the Netherlands. The French art dealer Jean-Baptiste Glomy (from whose name the term was derived) is thought to have been the first to produce work (often border-framing for prints) in this style, although the Dutch artist Zeuner (fl. 1773–1810) became its most famous exponent.

Chinese mirror painting of a female figure in a pastoral landscape, the subject probably derived from contemporary European engravings. The details of foliage and architecture, however, are of Chinese inspiration. About 1760.

BRISTOL

A coloured lead glass, produced at Bristol and by major factories throughout England c. 1760–1825, although now referred to as Bristol indiscriminately. Blue was the most popular colour, others being deep green, amethyst and very rarely dark red. The colours were created by the addition of metal oxides and they vary in intensity according to the quantities employed. Early examples consist largely of scent bottles, small boxes and luxury wares, but by c. 1770 decanters, finger bowls, drinking glasses, cruets, jugs and other domestic articles were manufactured widely. Decoration is usually simple, although fine and early pieces display elaborate gilding and enamelling.

Above "Bristol" glass, in characteristic blue, green and amethyst colours. English, c. 1770–1825.

NAILSEA

This distinctive range of inexpensive domestic and decorative wares was produced about 1790–1890 by factories throughout Britain and not limited to the Nailsea works in Somerset. There are three stylistic categories. First is the early "bottle and window glass" – jugs, vases, bowls, bottles and friggers coloured from palest green to dark olive and decorated with flecks and loops of white and coloured glass, and enamel. These were produced by window and bottle factories c. 1790–1830, to provide cheap domestic wares at a time when lead glass was still harshly taxed (until 1845).

Then there are the opaque white lead glass flasks, pipes, bells and other friggers, decorated with brightly coloured festoons (wavy or zig-zag) and produced by numerous lead glass factories after c. 1845.

The colourless lead glass carafes, walking sticks and other friggers decorated in filigree style (coloured glass threads twisted and embedded within the metal itself) are considered the most sophisticated of "Nailsea" styles; they too were produced after c. 1845.

"Nailsea" was also adopted contemporaneously in the U.S.A., especially in the south of New Jersey, although there existed earlier manifestations of the style in the 16th to 18th centuries in southern Spain, France and Germany.

Below Nailsea. The flask dates from c. 1850 (5in). The bottles are mottled with flecks of white and red enamel. This early manifestation of the style is often associated with the Shropshire factory of Wrockwardine Wood. About 1790–1830; height of gin-shaped bottle (*left*) 6½in.

Biedermeier: a beaker painted with transparent enamels, depicting the Karlskirche, Vienna, in the style of Samuel and Gottlob Mohn, Austrian, c. 1830.

BIEDERMEIER

The term "Biedermeier" has been used since the late 19th century to describe the fashionable artistic styles of Germany, Bohemia and Austria about 1815–45, a period which witnessed a revival of fine glass-making in northern Europe patronised by the newly established bourgeoisie. Large numbers of thick-walled goblets, beakers, tankards, vases and bottles were produced in lavish styles – cut profusely and engraved with picturesque views and portraits; flashed, stained and overlaid in brilliant colours; and enamelled in translucent shades depicting naturalistic floral bouquets, allegories and emblems. New styles were invented in keeping with current tastes, such as black Hyalith, and rich Lithyalin in imitation of semi-precious stones (developed by Frederick Egermann), and the yellow-green uranium glass called *Annagelb* and *Annagrün* (see Vaseline, below). Outstanding decorators of the period were Gottlob Mohn, Anton Kothgasser, Dominik Biemann (all of whom worked in Vienna) and August Böhm.

OPALINE

Opaline is a semi-opaque translucent glass, often of "milk and water" appearance or coloured, produced in France 1825–70 at Baccarat (where the term *opalin* was first used

c. 1823), Saint-Louis, Le Creusot, Choisy-le-Roi, Bercy and other factories. Early wares – vases, carafes and boxes – were of elegant form and proportion, frequently ormolu-mounted and of subtle shades. After about 1835, surfaces were sometimes enamelled and/or gilded, and as production increased to meet demand the range of opaline extended to include a variety of domestic wares. Special colours were: *gorge de pigeon* ("pigeon's neck": translucent mauve); *bulles de savon* (soap bubbles: delicate rainbow hues); yellow, turquoise and violet. White, bright greens and blues were more common.

In England, opaline was manufactured in the 1840s and 1850s by Richardson of Stourbridge (painted and gilded with classical scenes, flowers, or with trailed decoration such as coiled serpents), George Bacchus of Birmingham (transfer-printed designs for cheaper wares), J. F. Christy, and Rice Harris of the Islington Glass Co.; and in the U.S.A. after c. 1830 by the Boston and Sandwich Glass Co. Since c. 1932 opaline manufacture has continued in Venice.

LACY
This short-lived but distinctive style of early mould-pressed glass is characterised by elaborate lace-like patterning and stippling over the entire surface of the object. The style was popular in the U.S.A. c. 1830–40, and produced by the Boston and Sandwich Glass Co. (hence, the common term

American lacy glass wares, c. 1830–40.

Left Vaseline glass: the fairy night lamp in graduating shades of opalescent cream to transparent yellow, on a clear press-moulded stand, English, c.1880–1900; the chocolate cup and saucer of *Annagrün* glass, cut, enamelled and gilded with floral scrolls, Bohemian, c. 1835–40.

Below Opaline glass from France and England decorated variously with enamelling, gilding and applied trailing. About 1830–50; yellow vases 7½in.

Right Slagware: the turquoise marbled vases decorated in relief with birds, and the purple pot with twisted rope motifs. All 19th century, English.

Below Cranberry glass, plain or decorated in characteristic style with applied clear glass "shells". English, 19th century.

Sandwich glass) and by other factories in New England and the Mid-West. Plates, jugs, compôtiers and other domestic wares were decorated with many hundreds of intricate low-relief designs, in clear and coloured glass. Similar lacy styles were adopted contemporaneously in France, Belgium and England.

VASELINE
Vaseline is so called for its oily, yellowish-green colour, produced by the addition of uranium to the batch. In the years 1835–1900, English and American Vaseline glass was frequently press-moulded into simple styles and shapes, including candlesticks, vases and small baskets with fluted sides. In Bohemia, opalescent yellow (*Annagelb*) or green uranium (*Annagrün*) glass was developed by Josef Riedel and manufactured c. 1830–48 with cut and gilded decoration.

SLAGWARE
Press-moulded, domestic and decorative glass of marbled or plain appearance, usually in shades of turquoise, blue, brown, mauve or dark purple, streaked with opaque white. Slagware was produced c. 1840–1900 in England, especially in the Midlands and industrial north (e.g. at the Gateshead factories of J. G. Sowerby and George Davidson, and the Sunderland firm of Henry Greener). As the name implies, waste slag (skimmed from molten steel) was mixed with the glass for the characteristic streaky effect.

Many examples bear a full set of Patent Office registration marks, making identification and dating possible. Until 1883 these were lozenge-shaped, containing in each corner the coded day, month and year of the design's registration, surmounted by the Class number (III) for glass. The marks were used to mark much pressed glass (and other wares) of the period. Manufacturer's trademarks, such as a peacock's head (Sowerby), or a lion on a battlement (Davidson) also appear. After 1884, Patent Office marks appeared as serial numbers. (For specific codes, see *19th Century British Glass*, by Hugh Wakefield.)

CRANBERRY
This transparent red glass, ranging from pale pink to bright cherry, was produced for middle-class markets throughout the 19th century in England (Midlands and Stourbridge areas) and in the U.S.A. after c. 1850. Sometimes described incorrectly as "ruby" glass, it is distinctive from this dark ink-red colour, which developed earlier in Bohemia, in shade and intensity.

Cranberry friggers and simple domestic wares were manufactured before c. 1845 (while glass taxes were still levied), the majority unadorned and with clear colourless handles, stems and feet. Thereafter, examples are more decorative, with trailed, enamelled and moulded ornamentation (e.g. applied shells and flowers) over the surface. Other pieces were overlaid and cut, in imitation of fashionable Bohemian styles. Cranberry tableware, much of it reproducing 19th-century styles, is manufactured today in Czechoslovakia and England.

CAMEO GLASS
The Roman technique was revived in England, France and Bohemia during the second half of the 19th century, using contemporary processes. A blank (i.e. undecorated shape) made of two or more layers of different coloured glass, blown and fused together, was immersed in hydrofluoric acid solution (discovered 1771) to remove the shine. After painting the design onto the surface with acid-resistant varnish, the object was dipped again into acid, and the unprotected background was eaten away while the varnished sections remained intact. The relief design was finally wheel-engraved, and/or cut and refined with hand tools to create subtleties of tone, depth and shade.

Vases, bowls, scent bottles and plaques of exquisite colour and decoration were created by leading designers in France (see Gallé; Daum), and in England by John Northwood and his son John Northwood II, George and Thomas Woodall, Joseph Locke and Frederick Carder (the latter two emigrating later to America). Between 1870 and 1920, these English craftsmen were employed by the Stourbridge firms of Thomas Webb, Stevens and Williams, and Hodgetts Richardson, where separate workshops were established for cameo decoration. The best pieces were signed by individual craftsmen, or marked with the manufacturer's name (e.g. Webb's Gem Cameo).

For earlier examples, see p. 39 on Roman and pp. 48, 199 on Chinese cameo glass.

MARY GREGORY
Glass enamelled with opaque white figures of children was produced in the U.S.A., England, Bohemia and elsewhere in Europe c. 1870–1900. The origin of the term is perplexing. It is known that a Mary Gregory worked for the Boston and Sandwich Glass Co. in the 1880s, but her particular connection with this style of glass remains undocumented. It is more likely that the distinctive decoration developed first in Bohemia and was afterwards adopted by factories in the U.S.A. (Pittsburgh, and New England areas) and England (in the Midlands and on Tyneside).

Mary Gregory decoration was executed frequently on cranberry, blue, green, amethyst and amber glass. The boy and girl figures are often portrayed in silhouette, catching butterflies or playing. The quality of enamelling varies considerably, from the white lustrous sheen and meticulous detailing of fine Bohemian examples, to sloppy execution and use of flesh-coloured tints in England. Reproductions are made in Czechoslovakia, and fakes have appeared recently, poorly painted, but executed on 19th-century glass.

Mary Gregory cylindrical vase of cranberry colour, enamelled in lustrous opaque white with a child holding a parasol in a leafy glade. Bohemian, c. 1880.

Right Fine cameo glass vase, the rich red ground having a double overlay of blue and white, carved delicately with naturalistic flowers and leaves. Signed "Thomas Webb and Sons Cameo", c. 1885.

Below Pair of Amberina vases, and water jug with "thumb-print" design, showing fine shading from pale yellow to rich red. English, c. 1885.

LATER ARTISTS AND

AMBERINA

A type of art glass distinguished by its colour shading from clear yellow or amber to deep red (usually darkening at the top of the piece), produced in blown, moulded or pressed styles. It was made c. 1883–1900 in the U.S.A. by New England Glass Co. (where Amberina was patented in 1883, by Joseph Locke), Mount Washington (where it was called Rose Amber), and Hobbs Brockunier, and revived after 1917 by Libbey Glass; in England by Sowerby's Ellison Glass Works; and in France by Baccarat from c. 1916 (in delicate shades, known as *rose teinte*), and revived c. 1940.

The characteristic colour effects were achieved by the presence of gold particles dispersed throughout the metal which, when re-heated at certain parts, turned or struck a deep red (or purple, if over-heated). Those parts which were not re-heated remained yellow, enabling the glass-maker to create subtle gradations of shade.

BURMESE

This type of art glass is distinguished by its near-opaque shading from pale greenish-yellow to rich pink (darkening at the top of the object), the colour gradations created under heat treatment and by the addition of gold, uranium and other oxides to the metal. Various table and decorative wares were produced c. 1885–1900 in either shiny or matt (i.e. acid-etched) finish, in the U.S.A. by Mount Washington Glass Co., New Bedford, Mass., where Burmese was first patented by Frederick Shirley; and in England by Thomas Webb of Stourbridge, under the name of Queen's Burmese.

Many Burmese glass centrepieces, vases, lampshades and fairy lamps were enamelled with figural scenes, flowers, animals and inscriptions.

PEACHBLOW

This American art glass is distinctive for its colour shading from cream to deep rosy peach (imitating Chinese ceramic glaze effects) with a shiny or matt (acid-etched) finish. Domestic and decorative objects with slight colour variations were manufactured in the 1880s and 1890s by Hobbs, Brockunier and Co. (the west Virginian makers of Wheeling Peach Blow, a cased glass consisting of an opaque white lining overlaid with transparent colours), Mount Washington, New England, and Boston and Sandwich factories. Many examples were enamelled and/or gilded over the surface.

Cased Peach Glass or Peach Bloom was also manufactured in England by Thomas Webb, and by Stevens and Williams; it was imitated crudely in Bohemia for export markets.

Right "Queen's Burmese" glass of matt finish, by Thomas Webb and Sons. The vases are enamelled with leaves in shades of green and brown. About 1890.

Right, below Peachblow glass by Thomas Webb and Sons, the large vase of matt satin finish, and the pair with shiny surfaces, all with gilded relief designs. Note the underlying opaque white glass at the rims. About 1885–90.

LATER ARTISTS AND

SATIN

This late 19th-century art glass is distinctive for its silky feel and matt finish produced by the treatment of hydrofluoric acid. Burmese and Peachblow glass fall into this category, but the term "satin" applies particularly to decorative and table wares of white overlaid with coloured glass, and adorned with subtle lozenge- or oval-shaped surface designs that are created by trapping air locks between the two layers to form regular patterns. Pieces with a pearly lustrous sheen are called Pearl Satin glass, or *Verre de Soie* ("silk glass"), as named by the Stourbridge firm Stevens and Williams. Numerous patents for Satin and Pearl Satin were granted to factories in the U.S.A., Bohemia and England in the 1880s.

ART NOUVEAU

Glass lent itself well to the concepts of this international style of the late 19th and early 20th centuries, translating and expressing its inherent characteristics into flowing, elongated shapes, asymmetrical contours, naturalistic designs and evocative colours. Leading designers in France included Eugène Rousseau, Auguste Legras, Eugène Michel, Émile Gallé and Daum Frères, the latter two

Below Satin glass with "quilted" or lozenge-shaped surface patterning, the vase having a pearly lustrous sheen ("Pearl Satin") and gilded design on the rim. English, late 19th century.

Right Art Nouveau vase of elongated form, wheel-engraved in relief with swirling leaves and flowers in delicate shades of pink, mauve and green, with *appliqués* on the foot; small vase of mottled green, blue and pink tone, with *appliqués* on the sides. By Daum Frères, late 19th–early 20th century.

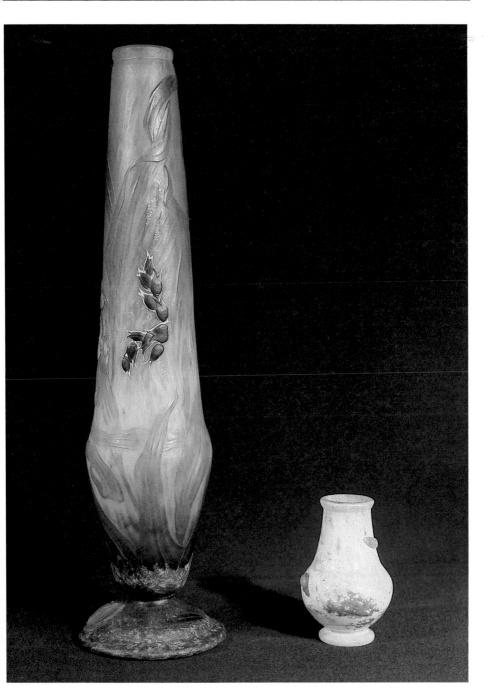

DECORATIVE STYLES

especially noted for their cameo vases displaying plant life, in delicate shades and fluid organic shapes. In the U.S.A., L. C. Tiffany's glass mosaic lamps and iridescent vessels reflected a new extravagance with their brilliant and lustrous surfaces and novel shapes, soon to be recalled in Austria by firms such as Loetz, Bakalowits and Palme-König. (See also Daum, Gallé, Lalique, Loetz, Tiffany.)

DAUM

The Daum Frères glass-works at Nancy, directed by the brothers Auguste and Antonin Daum, produced Art Nouveau glass 1889–1914 in the manner of Émile Gallé. Examples were adorned with naturalistic designs (landscapes, flowers, fruit, etc.) enamelled, acid-etched, applied or in cameo relief, frequently in muted shades. Vessel shapes reflected the attenuated, asymmetrical lines of Art Nouveau, or were derived from Islamic prototypes such as the long-necked bottle or "Berluze" re-created exclusively by Daum. Vases, and lamps with moulded glass shades and wrought-iron mounts in the form of mushrooms or flowers, were most popular.

Since c.1925 the firm has produced glass in a wide variety of decorative styles, sometimes incorporating the designs of contemporary artists such as Salvador Dali. Signatures vary according to period. Art Nouveau pieces were often signed "Daum, Nancy", with the Cross of Lorraine.

GALLÉ

Émile Gallé (1846–1904), the outstanding French designer and innovator, produced a wide and imaginative range of glass from about 1874. Initially inspired by classical, Islamic and Venetian prototypes, Gallé later absorbed Art Nouveau concepts to develop a highly personal style. The objects (mostly vases, bowls and lamps) reflect Gallé's close adherence to nature – marine life, flowers, plants, insects, etc. – transformed into fluid, elongated shapes and delicate surface patterns. Most popular were the cameo pieces decorated with naturalistic relief designs in two or more layers of different coloured glass (such as the highly favoured grey and amethyst combination) produced in large numbers at his Nancy factory from c.1890. Throughout his career, Gallé experimented with new colour techniques and special effects (using air bubbles, metal foils, etc.) and exerted an enormous influence on contemporary glass-making.

Examples are invariably signed, in a variety of styles. The factory continued production of signed cameo vases long after Gallé's death.

LOETZ

During the 1880s, this Austro-Bohemian firm (bought by Johann Loetz c. 1840) specialised in glass made to imitate semi-precious stones (e.g. aventurine and agate). Between about 1890 and 1900 iridescent glass – the most typical Loetz ware – was manufactured and exported most successfully, in response to the enormous popularity of Tiffany's Favrile. The fine lustrous wares, designed in the Art Nouveau taste, are distinctive for their abstract surface patterns and fluid, asymmetrical forms. After c. 1900,

Art Nouveau vases by Loetz, their flowing iridescent surface patterns reminiscent of Tiffany's Favrile glass. About 1890–1900.

iridescent glass was superseded by austere monochrome designs in the *Sezession* style of Vienna. Pieces were not always marked, although export wares were signed "Loetz Austria", while those for home markets were sometimes marked "Loetz Klostermühle" (the town) with crossed arrows in a circle. Production halted c. 1914, and was later revived briefly until 1932.

TIFFANY

Together with his associates Arthur and Douglas Nash, the highly acclaimed and influential American glass designer and manufacturer Louis Comfort Tiffany (1848–1933) developed new artistic styles in the Art Nouveau taste. A wide range of decorative vessels, stained glass windows and, notably, lamps were produced for luxury markets at his factories in New York c. 1895–1928. Particularly successful was the hand-made Favrile range, consisting chiefly of vases, and characterised by brilliant iridescence and shimmering surface effects created by spraying the hot exterior with metallic salts, which were absorbed into the metal (in imitation of buried and weathered ancient glass). Pieces are coloured in lustrous shades of blue, green, gold and pink, often adorned with peacock feathers, swirled and combed threads and naturalistic flowers. Other distinctive styles include Reactive glass (of fluorescent rainbow hues) and Aquamarine (of transparent sea-green colour, embedded with forms from aquatic and marine life).

Tiffany glasswares are marked variously; common signatures include "L.C.T.", "L.C. Tiffany/Favrile" ("Fabrile" before c. 1894) and "Louis C. Tiffany/Favrile". An inventory number and letter (coded to indicate the retail outlet) were also added. For further details, see *American Art Nouveau Glass* by A.C. Revi. (See also Loetz; Art Nouveau.)

CARNIVAL

This cheap pressed iridised glass is so-called because it was sold and given away at fairs and carnivals, and hence sometimes also called, because of its appearance, "poor man's Tiffany". It was mass-produced c. 1907–25 in the U.S.A. by Fenton Art Glass Co., Imperial Glass Co. (examples marked "Imperial" or with crossed arrows), Northwood Glass Co. (marked "N") and Millersburg Glass Co. A thick and heavier carnival glass was made by factories in northeast England in the 1920s and 1930s, and contemporaneously in Australia, by the Crystal Glass Co., and the Australian Glassworks.

Carnival lustres appear predominantly in shades of gold and "marigold" (orange), although Australian examples can usually be distinguished by darker colouring, including

a deep purple tint. Tablewares decorated with flowers, leaves and geometric motifs (among many others) and mottoes were popular.

ART DECO
Glass in this distinctive international style of the1920s and 1930s, which embraced both fine and applied arts, is enormously varied but general characteristics include a tendency towards angularity, both in form and decoration; the play and repetition of geometric shapes, and stylised surface motifs such as greyhounds, racing cars and female nudes; and a desire for novelty, transforming ordinary domestic wares into new and interesting shapes. Among the outstanding glass designers of the period were Maurice Marinot, François Décorchement, Gabriel Argy-Rousseau, René Lalique, Jean Sala and André Thuret (France); Keith Murray (for Stevens and Williams, England); Frederick

Favrile vases and stem cup (the latter in imitation of Roman glass) by Louis Comfort Tiffany, in iridescent shades of peacock blue, pink and gold. Late 19th–early 20th century.

American carnival glass dish decorated with the "peacock on the fence" pattern in shades of purple and turquoise. By Northwood Glass Co., first quarter of the 20th century.

Carder and Sidney Waugh (for Steuben Glass Works, U.S.A.); Sverre Pettersen (for Hadelands Glassverk, Norway); and Wilhelm von Eiff (Germany). Leading factories included Venini and Co. (Italy); Baccarat, and Daum (France); Orrefors (Sweden); Val St. Lambert (Belgium); and J. and L. Lobmeyr (Austria).

Art Deco decanters in bold geometric style, in keeping with "modernist" tastes of the 1920s–1930s.

233

LALIQUE

René Lalique (1860–1945) manufactured a wide and imaginative range of decorative wares including vases, statuettes, car mascots, scent bottles, desk accessories and lamps. Mass-produced at his factories in France c. 1908–45, and exported in quantity, Lalique's glass reflects the exuberant spirit of Art Deco and modernist ideals. The moulded pieces, boldly patterned and offered in a range of pale opalescent hues or vibrant colours, were reasonably priced through mass-production, resulting in an immense popularity. Each piece is marked "R. Lalique" (or very occasionally "Lalique"), etched, sand-blasted or moulded on the base or side.

Since 1946, production has continued under the name Cristallerie Lalique et Cie. Later examples can be distinguished by their "frosty" appearance, no longer hand-stained, enamelled, or of opalescent and coloured glass. The initial "R" is usually omitted from the mark; a few pieces made since 1946 retain it, through use of the old moulds.

VAL-SAINT-LAMBERT

An acclaimed manufacturer of crystal and art glass in Belgium, the Cristalleries du Val-Saint-Lambert were originally founded in 1825, near Liège, to imitate French, Bohemian and English styles. After 1890 fine and imaginative glass in the Art Nouveau, and later Art Deco, tastes was produced. Throughout the 20th century, the factory has employed leading designers such as Charles Graffart (joined 1906, and best remembered for his engraved pieces) and René Delvenne (from 1925), both later becoming artistic directors. Decorative glass, tablewares and paperweights have all been manufactured in a wide range of styles – cut, engraved, flashed and more

Top Moulded glass vases and dragonfly car mascot (*Grande libellule*) by René Lalique. The vases are decorated with stylise[d] motifs. Late 1920s–1930s.

Above Pâte-de-cristal pieces in Art Deco taste by Gabriel Argy-Rousseau (b.1885); a clearer and more resonant form of *pâte-de-verre*.

recently of surprising thickness, with abstract surface designs in exquisite colours.

Pieces are marked "Val St. Lambert" (or an abbreviation of this, sometimes also with designer's initials), usually incised on the base.

Left Blue vase of thickly cased glass, decorated over the surface with a swirling abstract design. By Val-Saint-Lambert, with engraved factory initials on the base, of recent manufacture; 12in.

Below Roman glass Janus flask and bowl displaying heavy and brilliant rainbow iridescence which is popular with collectors today. 1st century BC–2nd century AD; 3in diameter.

COLLECTING

The field of glass is an exciting and accessible one. There is an almost unlimited range of objects of every size, shape, colour, origin and price. This provides the collector with an enormous scope of categories from which to specialise, and the exporting of glass that has occurred since earliest times has resulted in the wide distribution of pieces throughout the world.

However, until recently the collecting of glass remained an unexploited area when compared to those of ceramics and metalware. This appears to have been a result of insufficient literature, poor documentation, the frequent absence on glass wares of makers' marks, and the presence of numerous fakes and reproductions – all of which contributed to a general difficulty in identification. These factors, together with the fragility of the medium and its subdued visual impact, have inhibited collectors, and restricted the expansion of the market for works of glass.

Despite the fact that these problems have not decreased significantly over the past ten years, interest has increased dramatically, as collectors have recognised the existence of a relatively inexpensive and undervalued field of antiques, one in which many pieces of the highest quality are still available for purchase. Of the wares illustrated in this book, the majority have been selected from auction houses and specialist dealers over a short period. They demonstrate the rich variety of glass available to the collector at any one time.

The difficulties outlined above may be overcome, to a large extent, with experience. The collector should view and *handle* pieces as often as possible, and compare examples with those on view in museums and shops in order to identify those characteristics fundamental to a particular style or period of manufacture. It is also important to seek

Selection of engraved 19th-century goblets, decorated variously with naturalistic ferns, flowers, palm trees and birds. Few collectors have recognised the quality and attractiveness of these period pieces, and examples remain accessible and inexpensive. About 1850–90.

the advice of experts and specialist dealers on the quality and authenticity of prospective purchases. A reputable dealer will always take back pieces which are later shown to be other than as sold, and is in the best position to locate further examples for your collection. The benefits of assured quality should outweigh the slightly higher prices charged by a specialist shop.

The careful examination of objects is essential, as most are not signed, and styles have been imitated widely from country to country and from one period to another. Various factors must be taken into consideration to establish the origin of the glass, its composition, method of manufacture, age and quality. This process of evaluation varies slightly from one category of glass to the next, but includes invariably an analysis of: form and shape; function; surface appearance (including patina or iridescence); colour; weight; and other external features such as decoration, and signs of wear. With a little experience, much can be deduced about the piece from such a visual assessment. For example, does the overall appearance of the object present a harmonious whole? If not, perhaps a handle or foot has been replaced. Does the purported period of manufacture match the purpose for which the object appears to have been made? If not, one or other, or both, must be incorrect. Does the iridescence appear too regular and smooth? If so, is there any reason to suppose it is not a fake? Does the alleged Roman glass weigh as little as it should, or does its heaviness suggest a later reproduction? Are the "Mary Gregory" figures executed with the skill which distinguishes the fine piece from the ordinary? A brief discussion of fakes and reproductions (and more on how to identify them) appears below.

PRICES AND DAMAGE

Prices for glass vary extensively from one category to the next, and the current values attached to different styles and periods may, at times, appear erratic and perplexing. An attractive but ordinary Roman glass vase dating to the 1st century AD might cost £100, while a unique Gallé vase may fetch over £50,000 at auction. Prices are not determined exclusively by the age of pieces, but also by comparative rarity, quality and aesthetic appeal. In addition, monetary values can fluctuate significantly as a result of current fashions and tastes, as demonstrated recently by the dramatic price rises for Art Nouveau and Art Deco glass, in keeping with the vogue for these international styles.

Over the last decade, prices have increased steadily. Nevertheless, there still exist many categories of glass which remain inexpensive and accessible, including

COLLECTING

Left Late 15th-century *Maigelein* (Lower Rhine) showing poor restoration: the section on the left side of the crack has been replaced with plastic (the standard material for glass repair) but its pale uneven colour contrasts sharply with the original green glass (seen on the right of the crack); in addition, the plastic surface has a gritty and oily feel.

Below Roman blue glass *Kantharos* showing good restoration: one of the spiral-twist handles has been re-created to replace the missing original – a sensitive and convincing match; part of the foot has been repaired similarly; and the cracked sides have been pieced together well, leaving no intervening spaces. 1st century AD; $4\frac{1}{8}$in.

ancient domestic objects of Far Eastern and Roman manufacture, Byzantine glass, and 18th- and 19th-century Anglo-Irish decanters and drinking glasses.

Condition plays an important role in the determination of price in all but the rarest pieces. It is a curious fact that many collectors demand perfection in glass, while collectors of ceramics, for example, will tolerate a certain amount of damage. A fine two-handled Roman glass cup would lose up to 80 per cent of its value if one of the handles had been replaced. On the other hand, if an unusual Roman cameo-cut glass bowl were cracked or chipped, its imperfect state would not necessarily be reflected by a lower price – in this case, rarity and fine workmanship make it a highly desirable purchase regardless of damage.

Not all replaced parts are considered unacceptable. For example, some four out of five English and Irish decanters found in the market today are missing their original stoppers. Nevertheless, if the replaced stopper is contemporary with the decanter in period, style and colour, its value will not be appreciably affected. This is also true of many chandeliers and candelabra in which cut glass lustres or whole branches have been replaced.

Small chips, such as those found commonly around the edges of drinking glasses and vessels, are not considered very serious if they do not mar the appearance or aesthetic appeal of the piece.

RESTORATION

The restoration of glass is a lengthy and delicate process, and should be undertaken only if necessary and by a reputable restorer. The *poor* repair of damage can reduce the value of the object significantly, and for this reason many small fractures and chips are not mended in order to preserve the shape, harmony and colour of the piece.

The majority of glass restorers will not accept direct commissions from private collectors, and damaged wares should be taken first to a reputable dealer who will advise on the importance of the damage, its relation to value, the scope and necessity for repair, and the costs involved. Restoration may include the grinding of small chips on the edge of the rim or foot, the piecing together of fragments or the replacement of a missing part.

CARE

Plain-surfaced glass should be washed in soapy, lukewarm water, and dried carefully to prevent damage of fragile parts, such as the stems of drinking glasses. Pieces decorated with enamelling and gilding should never be scrubbed, as the decoration can chip or rub off easily. Wet objects should always be dried immediately, as the water can stain the

Left A curious "marriage" goblet, composed of four distinct parts: the cup is the bottom of a splayed vase, probably of late mediaeval origin; below this is the base of a stemmed goblet dating to the 4th–6th centuries AD; the stem is probably from a 16th-century wine glass; and the foot is the reversed mouth of a Roman *unguentarium*.

Below right A three-handled beaker with dark turquoise trailing around the sides, displaying slight iridescence. Egypt, 3rd century AD. And (*left*) a modern forgery, made during the early 20th century at Hebron, Jerusalem. Note the clear shiny surface, and crudely applied trailing in bright turquoise.

glass. In addition, water left standing in a vase or vessel for a long period can harm the surface, biting into it or leaving behind a nasty deposit, depending on the composition of the piece. A common example of such damage is the misty bloom left behind in a decanter after it has been emptied of its contents. This can often be removed with a common household bleach, or it can be treated professionally by repolishing the interior surface with acid. The latter method must be carried out by an expert, as the acid can seriously harm the glass.

Pieces should never be displayed in direct sunlight, which can affect the composition of the glass, causing it to expand and fracture (especially at the handles and other delicate areas). Colourless glass can also develop a surface-deep greyish tinge when kept in sunlight for a long period of time, although coloured specimens are little affected. Finally, a damp environment should be avoided, particularly in the case of crizzled pieces, which require a dry atmosphere and moderate room temperatures.

FAKES

There are numerous fakes in the market today, some of which can be identified readily, while others are so convincing that experts remain confused. The majority are of 20th-century date and of one of two kinds. Some are a complete reconstruction of an original, made by using an identical or similar glass-making process and copying, with varying degrees of success, form, decoration and signs of age. The other fakes most commonly encountered involve the addition to the surface of a plain but *genuine* vessel new decoration, with the aim of increasing its potential value. In both cases, a fake is produced with the deliberate intent to deceive, unlike the reproduction, which is made to meet the growing demand for a particular style of glass, or in a spirit of experiment, or out of respect for the past.

The following paragraphs should be read in conjunction with those passages in the book which describe the original styles.

Reconstructions
Ancient Egyptian glass. Small brightly coloured vessels have been produced in imitation of genuine core-formed examples. Commonly, they are blown thickly and drilled through the top to copy the small apertures and density of the originals.
Roman glass. Fake domestic wares can often be identified by: weight – blown Roman glass is almost feather-light, while fakes tend to be comparatively heavy; pontil marks – before AD c. 250, the majority of vessels had their pontil

marks removed from the base – many reconstructions, however, such as those purporting to be of 1st-century Sidonian manufacture, display pontil marks, and their presence on early wares should be regarded with suspicion; decoration; iridescence and patina – the natural devitrification of the glass can be faked by exposing the surface to acid – true patina should lift off on the fingers; learn to recognise those categories of ancient glass which display iridescence or patina, and those which do not; dirt – often added in excess to the glass to convey authenticity.

Stained glass. Fifteenth-, 16th- and 17th-century leaded roundels have been faked. They can usually be identified by: the appearance of modern glass, possessing a regular smooth surface and refracting the light uniformly, unlike old glass with its impurities, air bubbles and varying thickness; smooth edges where the glass has been cut, unlike the rough grozing characteristic of genuine examples; the lack, or faking, of surface corrosion, imitated by drilling small holes into the glass, or splattering the surface with paint and dirt.

Venetian glass. Many convincing fakes, purporting to be of Renaissance manufacture, have been produced in Venice in recent years.

British Isles. Common forgeries include opaque white glass (e.g. decanters) in the style of James Giles, gilded and enamelled crudely with swags, flowers and other neo-classical motifs; mould-blown Irish decanters and tablewares made in reproduction moulds and marked with the Cork factory name (however, the CORK lettering appears too large and bold); and 18th-century drinking glasses and other wares. The latter should be examined carefully. The feet on genuine examples were sheared, displaying a sharp cut edge, while the edge on fakes is rounded, due to the flattening of the glass on a hard surface. Always look for signs of manufacture such as a small bump at the rim (the point at which cutting terminated), straight-lined ridges (left by the tongs), and swirls on the body (due to the natural cooling of the glass); fakes rarely show signs of the actual working of the metal, appearing too perfect and consistent. Old lead glass possesses a subtle lustre, and a pale greyish or yellowish tinge, while forgeries are distinctive for their brilliance, shine and clarity. Finally, inspect the cut edge of the foot for fine and irregular scratches, almost frosted in appearance: fake scratches appear too uniform, often executed in only one direction.

Decoration on genuine pieces

Examples of this type of fake include Roman domestic wares which have been engraved in a manner which is not in keeping with the function and/or style of the object

Reichsadlerhumpen, a 19th-century reproduction dated "1599". Unlike early examples (see illustration p. 61), the coloured enamels appear harsh in tone; the gilded band around the top is flat and uniform (originally, the gold was applied in sections, creating a slightly textured effect); and the glass is thick and heavy.

(many are sold too cheaply, at about one tenth of the value of authentic examples); 18th-century Dutch and English drinking glasses which have been engraved (often poorly) with genre scenes in the style of well-known artists, or with Jacobite emblems; and "Mary Gregory" glass, enamelled in opaque white on Victorian tinted glass, but not achieving the subtlety of tone and detailing of genuine examples.

REPRODUCTIONS
Many excellent reproductions were made throughout Europe (especially in Venice and Nuremberg) during the 19th century, in keeping with the vogue for historic revivals, and to meet the demands of the wealthy bourgeoisie for fine glass. Roman reliquary urns and cast *millefiori* bowls, Islamic mosque lamps, German enamelled *Humpen* and drinking glasses, Bohemian brandy flasks, Venetian *cristallo* decorative objects and nefs, have all been reproduced with care (and in some cases the method of manufacture employed was identical to that used for the prototype). Due to the problems of identification, the collector should seek the advice of reputable dealers, whose experience and knowledge can best distinguish between the genuine article, reproduction and fake.

BIBLIOGRAPHY

Victor Arwas, *Art Deco*, 1980
Douglas Ash, *Dictionary of British Antique Glass*, 1975
John Ayers, "Chinese Glass", *Transactions of the Oriental Ceramic Society*, Vol. 35, 1963–4
E. Barrington Haynes, *Glass Through the Ages*, 1948
Percy Bate, *English Table Glass*, 1905
Geoffrey Beard, *Modern Glass*, 1968
Vivienne Becker, *Antique and 20th Century Jewellery*, 1980
Janine Bloch-Dermant, *The Art of French Glass, 1860–1914*, 1980
British Museum (compiled by D. B. Harden, Hugh Tait and others), *Masterpieces of Glass*, 1968
British Museum, *Jewellery Through 7000 Years*, 1976
John A. Brooks, *Glass*, 1975
Francis Buckley, *A History of Old English Glass*, 1925
S. W. Bushell, *Chinese Art* (Volume II, Victoria and Albert Museum Handbook), 1919
Corning Museum of Glass, *Glassmaking, America's First Industry*, 1976
Sidney Crompton (ed.), *English Glass*, 1967
Derek C. Davis, *English Bottles and Decanters 1650–1900*, 1972
Derek C. Davis and Keith Middlemas, *Coloured Glass*, 1968
Frank Davis, *Antique Glass and Glass Collecting*, 1973
Alastair Duncan, *Tiffany Windows*, 1980
Charles Ede, *Collecting Antiquities*, 1976
E. M. Elville, *The Collector's Dictionary of Glass*, 1961, reprinted 1967
John Fleming and Hugh Honour, *The Penguin Dictionary of Decorative Arts*, 1977
Poul Fossing, *Glass Vessels Before Glass-blowing*, 1940
Kate Foster, *Scent Bottles*, 1966
Alice Wilson Frothingham, *Spanish Glass*, 1963
Philippe Garner (ed.), *Phaidon Encyclopedia of Decorative Arts 1890–1940*, 1978
Eleanor S. Godfrey, *The Development of English Glass-making 1560–1640*, 1976
Paul Hollister, *Glass Paperweights, An Old Craft Revived*, 1975
Paul Hollister, *Glass Paperweights of the New York Historical Society*, 1974
W. B. Honey, *Glass* (Victoria and Albert Museum Handbook), 1946
G. Bernard Hughes, *English, Scottish and Irish Table Glass*, 1956
Ruth Hurst Vose, *Glass*, 1975
S. E. Janson, *Glass Technology* (London Science Museum catalogue), 1969

R. Soame Jenyns and William Watson, *Chinese Art (The Minor Arts)*, 1966, reprinted as *Chinese Art, Textiles, Glass and Painting on Glass . . .*, 1980
Patricia McCawley, *Glass Paperweights*, 1975
George S. and Helen McKearin, *American Glass*, 1941
Roy Morgan, *Sealed Bottles, Their History and Evolution 1630–1930*, 1976
Barbara Morris, *Victorian Table Glass and Ornaments*, 1978
Katharine Morrison McClinton, *Lalique For Collectors*, 1975
Frederic Neuburg, *Glass In Antiquity*, 1949
Frederic Neuburg, *Ancient Glass*, 1962
Harold Newman, *An Illustrated Dictionary of Glass*, 1977
Barbara Norman, *Engraving and Decorating Glass*, 1972
Adeline Pepper, *The Glass Gaffers of New Jersey*, 1971
Ada Polak, *Glass, Its Makers and Its Public*, 1975
Albert Christian Revi, *American Art Nouveau Glass*, 1968
Axel von Saldern, *German Enamelled Glass*, 1965
Axel von Saldern, *Ancient Glass in the Museum of Fine Arts Boston*, 1968
George Savage, *Glass*, 1965
Deborah Stratton, *Mugs and Tankards, A Collector's Guide*, 1975
Hugh Tait, *The Golden Age of Venetian Glass* (British Museum), 1979
W. A. Thorpe, *A History of English and Irish Glass*, 1929
Christopher Vane Percy, *The Glass of Lalique, A Collector's Guide*, 1977
Victoria and Albert Museum, *Bohemian Glass*, 1965
Keith Vincent, *Nailsea Glass*, 1975
Hugh Wakefield, *19th Century British Glass*, 1961
Phelps Warren, "Later Chinese Glass 1650–1900", *Journal of Glass Studies*, Vol. 19, 1977
M. S. D. Westropp, *Irish Glass*, 1920, 2nd revised edition 1978
Geoffrey Wills, *Victorian Glass*, 1976
Harriet Wynter and Anthony Turner, *Scientific Instruments*, 1975

GLOSSARY

Air bubbles. Appear particularly on early soda glass vessels and stained glass windows; more recently used for decorative purposes.

Anglo-Irish style. A general term describing luxury moulded and cut glass wares popular in England and Ireland c. 1780–1825.

Annealing. An essential glass-making process: controlled re-heating and gradual cooling of finished wares, to remove internal stress and strengthen structure.

Applied decoration. A form of relief ornamentation, by adding to the vessel's surface glass threads, trails, blobs, prunts and other motifs.

Art glass. A general term to describe late 19th- and 20th-century decorative glass, including wares displaying special colour and surface effects.

At the lamp. The shaping of objects and ornaments from glass rods, using the flame of an oil lamp or Bunsen burner.

Baluster. Early English drinking glass, resting on a stem of baluster (slender above, swelling below) or inverted baluster form, often with knops. Baluster stems also appear on continental vessels and drinking glasses. *Balustroids* are later, lighter and taller (*see* pp. 98–9).

Batch. The mixture of prepared and measured glass-making ingredients, ready for melting.

Blank. A plain-surfaced object, before subsequent adornment.

Blow-pipe (or blow-iron). A hollow iron rod (about $5\frac{1}{2}$ feet long), the thick end used to gather a blob of molten glass, the other with mouth-piece for blowing, to shape the object.

Bottle glass. Unrefined glass, naturally dark green or brown, used for 17th-century English bottles, and early "Nailsea" domestic wares.

Brilliant style. A form of cutting glass profusely and elaborately over the whole surface, popular chiefly in America c. 1880–1910.

Cameo glass. Glass layered, or cased, and the outer layer(s) then removed in part, to create designs in relief against a background of contrasting colour.

Cased glass. Glass composed of two or more fused layers (or casings) usually of different colours, as used for cameo decoration.

Cold-painting. Painting on glass with lacquer- or oil-based pigments, with no subsequent firing.

Combed decoration. Glass threads applied to an object's surface, pulled with a pointed tool to form wavy, zig-zag and other patterns, and marvered flat; as found on ancient Egyptian glass.

Core-forming (or -winding). An ancient technique of covering a mud core with molten glass to form the vessel.

248

After annealing, the core was withdrawn.

Cristallo. Venetian soda glass, rendered colourless; so-called for its resemblance to rock-crystal.

Crizzling. The degeneration of glass, usually due to inaccurate mixing of ingredients – sometimes called "diseased" glass.

Crystal. A general term for fine quality clear glass; pieces so labelled today must contain a minimum amount of lead oxide under EEC regulations.

Cullet. Broken pieces of glass added to the batch; melts readily, saving fuel and material costs.

Drops. Blobs of glass applied for decoration and/or to facilitate holding; *or* cut glass ornaments or lustres hung from chandeliers; candelabra, etc.

Églomisé. The decorative application of gold or silver leaf to a glass surface, prior to engraving. The decoration was protected by varnish, foil or glass.

Enamels. Finely powdered glass and metallic oxides mixed with, e.g. oil, painted onto glass and subsequently fired.

End of day glass. Objects (e.g. friggers) made from molten glass left over in the factory pots at the end of the day.

Engraving. The decorative incision of the surface by use of wheels (*wheel-engraving*) or of diamond- or sharp-pointed tools (*diamond-point engraving*) to make linear or dotted (*stipple-engraving*) designs.

Etching. A decorative technique of incising the surface or rendering it shiny, matt or frosted, by exposure to hydrofluoric acid.

Faceting. The decorative grinding of a surface to create shallow diamonds, squares and other shapes.

Façon de Venise. Venetian-style glass, produced throughout Europe during the 16th and 17th centuries.

Filigree. (Italian: *filigrana*, "thread-grained".) A decorative technique of embedding and twisting white and coloured threads within the clear metal itself.

Finial. An ornamental and/or functional knob of various forms surmounting a decorative object or vessel.

Firing. The process of melting the batch; *or* re-heating the object to shape and/or decorate; *or* re-heating the object to fuse enamels and/or gilding to the surface.

Flashing. Decorative process of dipping a clear or coloured glass object into molten glass of a contrasting shade, then cutting through the thin "flashing" to create design.

Flux. An essential glass-making ingredient, such as plant ash (alkali), added to the batch which lowers the fusion point of the silica.

Forest glass. Domestic, greenish-coloured glass produced in forest glass-houses of Europe, in mediaeval and later times. Also called *verre de fougère* (France) and *Waldglas* (Germany).

GLOSSARY

Free-blowing. The forming of objects on the blow-pipe, by blowing and manipulating the hot, ductile glass.

Friggers. Objects produced throughout the 19th century in England and America as "end-of-day" wares, or by apprentices, often amusing and frivolous; similar pieces produced earlier in Spain.

Frit. Selected pre-heated glass ingredients, cooled, ground into a powder and added to the batch to facilitate fusion.

Gather. The blob of molten glass taken from the furnace pot on the tip of the blow-pipe or pontil for blowing or moulding.

Gilding. Decorating glass by using gold-based pigment, powder or gold-leaf, which might subsequently be fired to the surface for permanence.

Ice glass. Glass, first made in Venice in the 16th century, resembling cracked ice; made by dipping object in cold water during blowing, or rolling it in splinters of glass.

Iridescence. Deterioration of glass caused by burial in damp soil, resulting in a flaky, rainbow-coloured surface (common on Roman glass). An effect employed by Tiffany, Loetz and others, by exposing the surface to metal oxides.

Kick. A concavity on the underside of the base of an object, ranging from a gentle indentation to a high point.

Knop. A decorative blob or protrusion appearing commonly on stems of drinking glasses, in various styles.

Latticino or latticinio. (Italian: *latte*, "milk".) A broad term, most appropriately applied to opaque white threads of filigree decoration.

Lead glass. Glass containing lead oxide, introduced c. 1676 by George Ravenscroft and distinctive for its weight, durability and brilliance.

Marvering. The process of rolling a mass of molten glass, still attached to the blow-pipe, on a hard flat surface, to make it uniform; also used to embed glass threads, blobs and other motifs into surface of object.

Merese. On wine glasses, a collar with sharp edge usually at the top or base of the stem.

Metal. Glass, in molten or hard state.

Millefiori. (Italian: "thousand flowers".) A process of decorating glass with slices of coloured canes arranged to resemble flowers by embedding them in a clear glass matrix or fusing them in a mould.

Mould-blowing. The forming of objects, and often their simultaneous decoration in low relief, by blowing molten glass into a mould.

Mould-pressing (or pressing). A mechanised process, developed c. 1827, whereby molten glass is poured into metal moulds and pressed with a plunger to form a smooth interior and an exterior impressed with the patterned design in low relief.

Overlaying. "Casing", i.e. superimposing on the surface of a glass object a further layer, usually of contrasting colour.

Pâte-de-verre. (French: "glass paste".) Crushed glass, flux and colouring agent fused and fired in a mould, to produce sculptural and unusual colour effects. Revived during the Art Nouveau period.

Pattern-moulding. Blowing molten glass into a mould, the interior of which is patterned.

Pillar-moulding. A popular Roman decoration of vertical ribs formed by working vessels (mainly bowls) while soft with pincers and other tools, or by moulding.

Pontil. An iron rod used for handling glass during manufacture, e.g. while shaping the partly formed object after it has been blown.

Pontil mark. The rough mark, found on the base of an object, where the pontil was removed.

Potash glass. A type of glass containing potassium carbonate (potash) derived from certain tree and plant ashes, manufactured in "forest" glass-houses of Europe.

Prunt. A blob of glass applied to the surface of an object (mainly drinking vessels) for decoration and to facilitate holding.

Rods. Sticks of glass, used for filigree decoration, or for making canes from which slices could be cut for *millefiori*.

Sand-blasting. A decorative technique of exposing glass to blasts of sand to render the surface matt and/or frosted.

Silica. An essential glass-making ingredient, derived from sand, river pebbles or powdered flints.

Soda glass. A type of glass containing sodium carbonate (soda) derived from marine-plant ashes, manufactured chiefly in Mediterranean areas; light and highly plastic.

Stippling. A decorative technique of tapping a glass surface gently with a pointed instrument to create design and tonal effects with tiny dots (stipples).

Striking. The careful re-heating of a glass object to develop certain colours and/or special effects (as used in making gold ruby glass and Amberina).

Tesserae. Small pieces of glass arranged and cemented into mosaic compositions; used to decorate interiors and in jewellery.

Threads. Slender strands of glass used in filigree patterns, twist stems, or applied decoratively to the exterior of an object as in "snake-thread" ornamentation.

Trailing. The decorative application of softened threads of glass to the surface of an object.

Twist. A type of decorative stem, found chiefly on 18th-century English drinking glasses, distinctive for white, coloured and/or air threads, twisted within the metal to create various elaborate designs.

Verre églomisé. See Églomisé.

ACKNOWLEDGEMENTS

Photographs were supplied by the American Museum in Britain, Bath on pp. 27, 92, 152, 187 (all on loan from the collection of the Henry Ford Museum), 90, 91, 141*l*, 217 (all on loan from the Corning Museum of Glass); "The Antique Collector", London 15, 56, 104, 124, 162, 170, 173*b*, 181*b*, 195, 203, 211, 215*br*, 237, 242*t*, 242*b*; British Museum, London 44, 55, 97; Christie, Manson & Woods, London 89; Cleveland Museum of Art, Ohio 87 (Leonard C. Hanna Jr. Collection); Cornell University, Herbert F. Johnson Museum 188; Corning Museum of Glass, New York 135*b*, 200*t*; Delomosne, London 70*t*, 70*b*, 74, 77, 129, 131, 137, 144*r*, 157*r*, 167, 168*t*, 169, 172*t*, 172*b*, 173*t*, 174, 177, 189*t*, 189*b*, 193; Fitzwilliam Museum, Cambridge 66 (courtesy of Delomosne), 126; Sonia Halliday, Weston Turville 208; Louvre, Paris 204; Museo Vetrario, Murano 171, 185 (photographs by Giacomelli, Venice); National Museum of Ireland, Dublin 132*r* (courtesy of Delomosne); Ann Ronan Picture Library, Loughton 7, 10, 26, 206; Sotheby Parke Bernet & Co., London 19*t*, 28, 30, 34, 35, 37*t*, 37*b*, 39, 42, 46, 51, 59, 64*l*, 67, 79, 113*t*, 123*t*, 132*l*, 156*t*, 156*b*, 157*l*, 158, 160*t*, 160*bl*, 175, 210; Sotheby Parke Bernet Inc., New York frontispiece, 95; Spink & Son, London 14; Toledo Museum of Art, Ohio 140*l* (Gift of Mr & Mrs G. Kirby); Victoria & Albert Museum, London 43, 53, 76, 81.

Glass was made available for photography by R.A. Barnes, London 78*t*, 108, 179, 216, 218*t*, 222, 223*t*, 223*b*, 225*t*, 225*b*, 226, 233; W. G. T. Burne, London 11, 75*b*, 113*b*, 121, 122*t*, 130, 139, 150, 153*t*, 155, 166, 168*b*, 185*tl*; Delmosne & Son, London 22, 105, 106, 114*t*, 115, 126, 135*t*, 138, 184, 186; Editions Graphiques, London 227, 228, 230, 232, 234, 235; Andrew Edmunds, London 151*t*; The Golden Past, London 200*b*; Harvey & Gore, London 197; Gerald Satin, London 117*b*, 123*b*, 140*t*, 159*t*, 160*br*, 238; Sheppard & Cooper, London 20, 24, 29, 32, 36, 57, 100, 101*b*, 119*tl*, 127, 145*t*, 148, 178, 240*t*, 240*b*, 245; Sotheby Parke Bernet & Co., London 17, 52, 61, 101*t*, 107, 110, 112*t*, 112*b*, 114*b*, 117*t*, 118, 119*tr*, 142, 144*b*, 151*b*, 153*b*, 159*b*, 180, 198; Spink & Son, London 49, 213; M. Thompson, London 19*b*, 21, 69, 71, 78*b*, 96, 99, 120, 141*t*, 145*b*, 147, 183*t*, 183*b*, 190, 214, 215*bl*, 219*t*, 219*b*; Mel Traub, London 218*b*; Vandekar, London 47, 64*tr*, 65*t*, 85, 149, 192; Victoria & Albert Museum, London 83, 84; other private collections 75*t*, 103, 236.

Special photography by Barnes & Bradforth, London 21, 69, 71, 78*b*, 96, 99, 120, 141*r*, 145*b*, 147, 190, 215*bl*; A.C. Cooper, London 151*t*, 197, 200*b*; Paul Forrester, London 22; Bay Hippisley, London 20, 57, 145*t*, 148; Graham

ACKNOWLEDGEMENTS

Portlock, Sawbridgeworth 11, 17, 19*b*, 24, 29, 30, 32, 36, 47, 49, 52, 61, 64*tr*, 64*b*, 65, 75*t*, 75*b*, 78*t*, 83, 84, 85, 88, 100, 101*t*, 101*b*, 103, 105, 106, 107, 108, 110, 112*t*, 112*b*, 113*b*, 114, 115, 116, 117*t*, 117*b*, 118, 119*r*, 121, 122*t*, 123*b*, 126, 127, 130, 135*t*, 138, 139, 140*r*, 142, 144*b*, 149, 150, 151*b*, 153*t*, 153*b*, 155, 159*t*, 159*b*, 160*br*, 166, 168*b*, 178, 179, 180, 181*t*, 183*t*, 183*b*, 184, 185*t*, 186, 192, 198, 213, 214, 216, 217, 218*t*, 218*b*, 219*t*, 219b, 222, 223*t*, 223*b*, 225*b*, 226, 233, 236, 238, 240*t*, 240*b*, 245; Rodney Todd-White, London 227, 228, 230, 232, 234, 235.

Line artwork by John Fuller; additional drawings by Miller Craig and Cocking; map by Liz Orrock.

The Publishers have attempted to observe the legal requirements with respect to the rights of the suppliers of photographic materials. Nevertheless persons who have claims are invited to apply to the Publishers.

INDEX